ArtScroll Series®

Rabbi Nosson Scherman / Rabbi Meir Zlotowitz

General Editors

ETERNAL

Published by
Mesorah Publications, ltd

ספר דרך אמונה

דרך אמונה בחרתי... (תהלים קיט:ל)

EMUNAH

A Torah Perspective of Achieving and Living with Faith

RABBI DOVID TZVI ELIACH

Translated by Rabbi Yehudah Bulman

FIRST EDITION
First Impression ... September 2003

Published and Distributed by
MESORAH PUBLICATIONS, LTD.
4401 Second Avenue / Brooklyn, N.Y 11232

Distributed in Europe by
LEHMANNS
Unit E, Viking Industrial Park
Rolling Mill Road
Jarow, Tyne & Wear, NE32 3DP
England

Distributed in Australia and New Zealand by
GOLDS WORLD OF JUDAICA
3-13 William Street
Balaclava, Melbourne 3183
Victoria, Australia

Distributed in Israel by
SIFRIATI / A. GITLER — BOOKS
6 Hayarkon Street
Bnei Brak 51127

Distributed in South Africa by
KOLLEL BOOKSHOP
Shop 8A Norwood Hypermarket
Norwood 2196, Johannesburg, South Africa

ARTSCROLL SERIES®
ETERNAL EMUNAH

ISBN:
1-57819-381-8 (hard cover)

Typography by CompuScribe at ArtScroll Studios, Ltd.

Printed in the United States of America by Noble Book Press Corp.
Bound by Sefercraft, Quality Bookbinders, Ltd., Brooklyn N.Y. 11232

לזכר ולעילוי נשמת
אבינו רועינו אציל המדות

הר״ר שמעון ב״ר שלמה זלמן ע״ה

שהיה דוגמא למופת של אמונה ובטחון בה׳
אמונת חכמים אהבת תורה ויר״ש
נפטר כ״ט תשרי תשד״מ

ת.נ.צ.ב.ה.

לכבוד אמנו היקרה תליט״א מנב״ת
שמסרה נפשה לגדל אותנו לתורה ויר״ש
והשרישה בנו יסודות האמונה ובטחון בה׳.

השי״ת יאריך ימי׳ ושנותי׳ בטוב ובנעימים
עד ביאת הגואל בב״א.

משפחת שפירא

RABBI MOSES FEINSTEIN
455 F. D. R. DRIVE
New York, N. Y. 10002

ORegon 7-1222

משה פיינשטיין
ר"מ תפארת ירושלים
בנוא יארק

בע"ה

הנה ראיתי כמה מהחלקים של הספר החשוב "דרך אמונה" וגם הספר "דרך עליה" על עניני השקפה והלכה שחיברו הרה"ג מוהר"ר דוד צבי אליאך שליט"א מירושלים עיה"ק. ואף שקשה לפני, מחמת טרדותי המרובות, לעבור על כל פרטי הספרים החשובים האלו, וממילא איני יכול לקבל אחריות לדבר כ"כ חשוב, מ"מ הכרתי איך שנכתבו הספרים להיות לתועלת, ליתן מוסגי התורה והיראה בליבם של הקוראים. והריני מברכו שיצליחהו השי"ת בדבר גדול זה, להגדיל תורה ולהאדירה לתפארת השם ותורתו, ויזכה לחבר עוד ספרים חשובים, ושע"י הפרצת אמונת תורתינו הקדושה נזכה בקרוב לביאת הגואל.

הכו"ח לכבוד התורה ולכבוד הרה"ג המחבר שליט"א ביום כ"ג סיון תשמ"א בנוא יארק.

משה פיינשטיין

משה פיינשטיין

RABBI I. J. WEISS

CHIEF RABBI
OF JERUSALEM

JERUSALEM, RECHOV YESHAYAHU 20

יצחק יעקב וויס

רב ואב״ד

לכל מקהלות האשכנזים פעיה״ק ירושלם תובב״א

מח״ס שו״ת מנחת יצחק

ירושלים, רחוב ישעיהו 20

בס״ד, ירושלים. עה״ק ת״ו, יום א׳ נצבים א׳ דסליחות כ״ב אלול תשמ״ח לפ״ק.

כן בא לפני האי צורבא מרבנן חוב״ט צמ״ס הרב הגאון מוה״ר דוד אליאך שליט״א מפה עיה״ק, ותלמודו בידו ספרו ״חידושי דוד״ ביאורים וחידושים בעניני הלל ושירה, והנה כבר אתמחי גברא ואתמחי קמיע בספריו היקרים אשר חיבר בעניני ראשית חכמה יראת ד׳, וראיתי דברי ידינ״פ הגה״צ הביד״צ דפעיה״ק שליט״א הרואים בספרו זה תועלת לרבים,

על כן אף ידי תיכון עמו וזרועי תאמצנו לברכו כי יתקבלו דבריו באהלי תורה ויראה, יפוצו מעיינותיו חוצה, מתוך נחת ובריאות איתנה, ונזכה לראות במהרה בהרמת קרן התורה וישראל, ולשנת גאולה וישועה, בבנין בית הבחירה, ברחמים רבים אכי״ר.

הכ״ד הכו״ח לכבוד התורה ולומדי׳
ומחכה לישועת ד׳ הקרובה

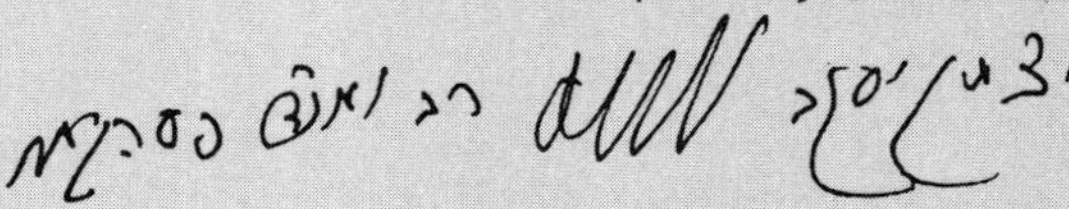

Rabbi SH. Z. AUERBACH
Jerusalem

הרב שלמה זלמן אויערבאך
פעיה"ק ירושלם תובב"א

ב"ה יום ג"א שבט תשל"ו

ישא ברכה מאת ד' האי גברא יקירא אשר יראת ד' היא אוצרו מע"כ הרה"ג
מוה"ר דוד צבי אליאך שליט"א   אחרי תת ברכה בכבוד ויקר
כיאות אודיעו שמלאתי מבוקשו ועיינתי מעט בספרו "דרך עליה" על דברי קנין
תורה ועבודה וראיתי בו דברים רבים אשר מאד הטבו בעיני והם יעידו על הכל
ובפרט שיודע אני את האיש ואת שיחו שכוונתו לשמים וכל רצונו לדבר על לב
האדם ולמשוך אותו ליראה את ד' ולאהבה אותו, וכמעשהו בספרו "דרך אמונה"
כך מעשהו בספר זה ועוד הוסיף לתת בו טעם לשבח בזה ששילב את הענינים
החשובים שבוא נו"נ בהם עם ביאורים ובירורים לאור ההלכה* והצליח לחדור
בתבונה באותם הענינים החשובים לחשוף ולברר את האמת הצפון בהם. אשר
על כן יאמינא לפעלא טבא יישר כחו וחילו לאורייתא ויזכהו ד' להרבות תורה
ויראת שמים ויפוצו מעינותיו חוצה ותרבה הדעת.

נאום שלמה זלמן אויערבאך

*) לצורך הענין הנני מוסר לו את אשר רשום אצלי מכבר בענין הלאו של לשון הרע

משה חברוני ראש הישיבה דישיבת חברון כנסת ישראל בעיה"ק ירושלם תובב"א ת. ד. 5162

Rabbi **MOSHE HEBRONI** Dean of the Hebron Yeshiva Knesset Israel P.O.B. 5162 JERUSALEM Israel

ב"ה. ירושלם ח' תשרי תשל"ה Jerusalem

הן בא לפני ידידי רב חביבי
הרב המו"ה ר' דוד אליאך שליט"א
משגיח רוחני של ישיבת איתרי בירושלים
וחיבורו בידו מאמרי חכמה ראשית
חכמה יראת ה'.
וכמעט שעיינתי ראיתי הרבה דברי חכמה
ושמח לבי בראותי שידידי עלה במעלה
רמה ביותר
וזכורני עוד כשלמד בישיבתנו היה
בצעירותו שהי' בחור שאנן רוח
ומצוין בתו' ומדות טובות
ובלי ספק שדברי חכמה המאירים
יהיו מאד מועילים למי שיש לו הבנה בחלק
התורה זו.
ויהי ה' עמו שיתגדל ספרו היקר
בי מדרשא ולפני כל בני תורה
הכו"ח

משה חברוני

אלעזר מנחם מן שך

קרית הישיבה

בני־ברק

אלעזר מנחם מן שך
ר״מ
ישיבת
פוניבז׳
בני־ברק. קרית־הישיבה

כאשר הראני כבוד ידידי הרה״ג יקר יקרים גדול בתורה וירא אמ״ר דוד אליאך שיחי׳ את אשר העלה על הכתב ממה שחידש במחשבת היראה ואם כי אינני מוסמך לבוא בהסכמה על ענינים העומדים ברומו של עולם, אולם ממה שראיתי ועיינתי קצת בהדברים האלו נוכחתי לדעת כי הם דברים השוים לכל נפש ובפרט לבני תורה אשר עיונם הוא שלא מקופיא,

וכל המעיין בהם ימצא טעם וחיזוק להוסיף ביראה ותורה, כי הדברים נאמרו בדעת תורה.

והנני לברכו שיזכה להפיץ מעינותיו כהנה וכהנה.

מנאי

אלעזר מנחם שך

יוסף שלום אלישיב
ירושלים

בס"ד [illegible]

לכבוד הרה"ג המופלג מוהר"ר דוד צבי הילמן שליט"א

ברכה ושלום רב.

הנני מאשר בזה קבלת ספרו היקר [illegible]

[illegible]

[illegible]

[illegible]

[illegible]

[illegible]

יהי רצון [illegible] ה' יצליח בידו [illegible]

[illegible]

[illegible]

בברכת התורה

יוסף שלום אלישיב

TABLE OF CONTENTS

Author's Preface to the English Edition

The original Hebrew version of this work, *Derech Emunah,* was written to spread and deepen *emunah* (faith) in our generation. This edition fills my long-standing desire to have it translated into English so that it can be distributed to an ever widening circle of communities. It is therefore with much gratitude that I give thanks to Hashem Yisbarach for leading me to this special moment.

Thank you to the staff of Artscroll publishers, and to its distinguished and energetic directors, Rabbi Meir Zlotowitz *shlita* and Rabbi Nosson Scherman *shlita,* for taking this endeavor upon themselves and seeing it to fruition.

Special thanks to my dear student and friend, Rabbi Lazer Spira נ"י of Boro Park, who conceived the idea of having this work translated. R' Lazer did not leave it as a "nice idea"; he dedicated himself to make sure it would be executed properly. He also took the responsibility of reviewing the entire manuscript for accuracy.

Thank you to Rabbi Yehudah Bulman נ"י, the son of my friend HaRav HaGaon Rabbi Nachman Bulman *zt"l,* for his clear and graceful translation.

May they all be blessed.

David Tzvi Eliach

Yerushalayim
Elul, 5763

Preface

This book first appeared in Hebrew as *Derech Emunah* — A Path to Faith, in 5735 (1975). But the idea to write this book came many years earlier. In my youth, my teachers and the books I read made me realize that the foundation upon which the Torah is founded and the goal of serving God is to arrive at a clear knowledge of God and to cling to Him. The prophet Chavakkuk summarized all the principles of Judaism in one phrase: "The righteous person shall live through his faith" (*Chavakkuk* 2:4).

Faith is the source of all the commandments, and it is the result of all the commandments, for "All of Your commandments are faith" (*Tehillim* 119:86). It is not enough, I was taught, to have a superficial knowledge of the principles of Torah faith; one must delve into its subtopics and drive them into one's heart, as the Torah says, "You shall realize it today and impress it upon your heart, that it is Hashem Who is God in Heaven above and on the earth below; there is none other" (*Devarim* 4:39).

At the time I decided to write this book, there were very few works on the topic; there were even fewer written for the average reader. Many people were writing *sefarim* on halachah and aggadah, but hardly any were interested in the essential topic of faith.

On the other hand, materialism and its twins — ignorance and heresy — were rampant (unfortunately, this has only gotten worse), and their preachers had many platforms and weapons in their arsenals. Too many people were falling (and continue to fall) into their traps or were imbibing their poison with abandon, without realizing that "all who come to her do not return" (*Mishlei* 2:19).

All this motivated me to write a book on the topic of faith using sources and a style that would be accessible to a wide audience of readers. My intent was to present a collection of firsthand sources from our rich heritage and to highlight often overlooked gems of *emunah* in God's wondrous deeds.

Still, I hesitated, Who am I to write such a book? But then I recalled the words of the Tanna: "You are not required to finish the task, yet you are not free to withdraw from it" (*Avos* 2:21), so I decided to attempt the task with the help of Heaven, with a prayer that He would help me complete the task. Perhaps, I hoped, others will also be encouraged to work on this project as well. In this way, I succeeded, with Hashem's help, to follow the adage of the wise man quoted by the author of the *Chovos HaLevavos*: "Part of caution is not to be too cautious" — if you wait to do something until you feel you can do it perfectly, you will never do it. Furthermore, I was inspired by the words of the Rambam, "It is more beloved in my eyes to teach about one of the principles of our religion and about faith than anything else I may teach" (*Rambam, Commentary* to the last Mishnah of *Berachos*).

I thank Hashem "Who graciously endows man with knowledge" for the kindness He showed me in my past — for leading me on a path of truth and faith; and I pray for the future that He save me from falsehood and heresy. I can only thank Him with the words of King David: "From Your hand have we given to You" (*I Divrei HaYamim* 29:14) — whatever I have accomplished is not mine; I am just returning what You gave me.

This volume is part of a larger work that also includes pathways to reaching higher levels of Divine service. Many *gedolim*, including HaRav Y. Y. Kanievsky *zt"l* and others, gave me much encouragement; may all their blessings be fulfilled.

I hereby acknowledge my deep gratitude to all my teachers and guides in life: to the Chevron Yeshivah of Yerushalayim; and, in particular, to my teacher R' Elyah Lopian *zt"l*, whom I merited serving; and to the great *tzaddik*, R' Yechezkel Levenstein *zt"l*. A very special thanks to my students "from whom I learned the most" (cf. *Taanis* 7a). May they all be blessed!

May it be the will of Hashem that the message contained in this book bear fruit for many generations to come, and "May our eyes behold Your return to Tzion in compassion," and may "the earth be as filled with knowledge of Hashem as water covers the seabed" (*Yeshayah* 11:9).

David Tzvi Eliach

Yerushalayim
Elul, 5763

CHAPTER ONE

On the Essence of Man

A. The body is the garment of the soul

A person is not the body — which we see — but the soul — which we cannot see. It is the soul that gives life to the body and activates it. And it is the soul that understands; knows; feels; and, in general, experiences. While the soul has no physical shape, it does have the same structure as the physical body, but in spiritual form: It, too, has 248 "limbs" and "organs"; and 365 spiritual "veins," "arteries," and "sinews."

The physical body is a garment tailored to the form of the soul, much like physical items of clothing are made to fit the needs of the body. Thus the soul is cloaked in the body. It then energizes the body and guides it — like an ax in the hand of a woodchopper — in whatever it does or senses. This is why when the soul departs, the body becomes a paralyzed, lifeless corpse: "Thus the dust returns to the ground, as it was, and the spirit returns to Hashem Who gave it" (*Koheles* 12:7).

B. The positive mitzvos are the soul's food

Just as the body needs food and air to live and flourish, so too, the soul needs "food" and "air" for nourishment. But since it is a spiritual entity, its food and air are also spiritual. What is its food? The positive mitzvos of the Torah. There are 248 positive mitzvos in the Torah, parallel to the soul's 248 limbs and organs. Indeed, each mitzvah has a counterpart limb or organ in the body that resembles the mitzvah in some way. Thus, there is a direct correlation between mitzvos and life — "You shall keep My statutes and laws which a person shall do and thereby live [forever]" (*Vayikra* 18:5)!

Everything in the universe was created by an utterance of the Creator, may He be blessed. In fact, everything that exists needs His constant flow of bounty for it to continue. This continued sustenance also comes from the "breath of the Creator's mouth," as is written, "Forever, Hashem, Your word stands firm in the heavens" (*Tehillim* 119:89). We therefore say in our morning prayers, "In His goodness He renews daily, perpetually, the work of creation. As it is said: '[Give thanks] to Him Who makes the great luminaries'" (ibid. 136:7) — "Who makes" is in the present tense. Likewise, the prophet Nechemia also used the present tense to convey that God continually gives life: "You give them all life" (*Nechemia* 9:6). But in order for man to receive this flow of sustenance, he must be connected to God. How does man connect to God? When he performs good deeds. Good deeds have the power to draw a holy, spiritual sustenance known as the "light of God," which shines upon the person and infuses his soul with life. Thus it is written, "In the light of the King's countenance is life" (*Mishlei* 16:15); and, accordingly, the blessing of "May Hashem show Himself to you in a shining countenance" (*Bamidbar* 6:25) can be understood as a blessing for life.

C. Sins cause spiritual illnesses in the "organs" of the soul

And just as the body has veins and arteries — conduits for the blood that transports the nourishment needed by the organs — so too, the soul has "veins" and "arteries." And just as the physical veins and arteries can become clogged or diseased if the person does not eat healthy and nourishing food, so too, the spiritual veins and arteries can become "clogged" or diseased. "Healthy food" for the soul is the positive mitzvos, and the "poisonous food" is the prohibitions of the negative mitzvos. There are 365 negative commandments, corresponding to the 365 "conduits" of the soul. This correspondence alludes to the fact that sins clog and block the "arteries" of the soul, preventing the spiritual "blood" from reaching the spiritual organs and cutting them off from the vital nourishment they need in order to live. Some sins can also actively poison and kill various organs of the soul. Finally, when a person's sins are very numerous, they can even kill his entire soul — just as a severe physical illness can kill an entire body.

D. Humans crave pleasure and dread losing it

It is natural for humans to seek pleasure. A man will not do anything unless he expects to get some benefit from doing the action. Yes, there are people who will live a life of privation, but only when they believe that the hardship is but a temporary "price" for ultimately achieving more lasting pleasure. People therefore crave expected pleasure — and call it good — and dread the lack or loss of pleasure — and call it bad.

E. People equate pleasure with goodness

How pleasure is measured is a purely subjective matter, of course, for each individual will measure pleasure in accord with his own tendencies, senses, and desires. And since people equate pleasure with goodness, what they judge as "good" or "bad" will also depend on their personal bent and on the intensity of what they consider pleasurable. This is why the concept of "good" varies between people and depends on such factors as age, intellect, and temperament or on the emotions of jealousy, passion, and glory seeking. For these are the roots of a person's desire, which in turn will guide his leisure and dictate on what he will spend his energy; the activities in which he will engage; and to what he will be sensitive. Children, for example, are drawn to childish games; most often, they are attracted more to games and other diversions than they are to activities that would be truly beneficial for their health (such as proper diet and appropriate relaxation) or for their future (such as going to school and learning in general). Adults, though, scorn the desires of children, which they consider petty, yet they take their own desires for food and drink etc. very seriously. Then there are adults who consider themselves more sophisticated than the average adult, so they will scorn other adults. To them, the pursuit of money and fame is what is really important. And so on.

As long as a person is not accustomed to true spiritual life and to spiritual food, he will think that the only good in the world is physical pleasure. He will also think that the only aspects of reality that exist are physical and corporeal things. Furthermore, such a person views belief in the existence of spirituality a fantasy and calls spirituality a myth. He looks down upon spiritual people with contempt. In his eyes, "the man of spirit is a fool" (cf. *Hoshea* 9:7), and "one who refrains from evil" is "foolish" (cf. *Yeshayah* 59:15). Sadly, he does not realize that in the eyes of someone who is truly wise, he is just a child, a fool, and an ignoramus!

F. Spiritual pleasure is infinitely greater than physical pleasure

The pleasure-craving person that we have just described would be much better off if he would know and accept the fact that the spiritual pleasure experienced by the soul and through its type of food is infinitely greater than any pleasure he can imagine. Compared to spiritual pleasure, if all the physical pleasures of the world could be weighed on a scale, they would not weigh as much as the thin peel of a head of garlic: "Better one hour of spiritual bliss in the World to Come than the entire life of this world!" (*Avos* 4:22).

G. Spiritual pleasure is limitless

In general, the more physical something is, the more limited it is; the more spiritual something is, the more unlimited it is. In space and time, this means that physical things take up a finite amount of space and only last for a limited duration. On the other hand, spiritual things are expansive and are not limited by the bounds of time and space. This can be observed even in our world, for some of the elements of the world are more spiritual than others, as follows. Everything in the world is comprised of four elements; if we list them in the order of less spiritual to more spiritual, they are: earth, water, wind, and fire. Earth, which is the lowest of the elements, can be divided into particles of dust, and is easily eroded. Water, which is above it, usually cannot be broken apart to such small parts but to droplets, which are larger and longer lasting (water can erode earth). Wind has vast "wings" and has the power to [evaporate water,] uproot mountains, and smash stones. And fire, which is the most spiritual of the elements, can spread and reduce even the strongest objects to ashes.

The same principle applies to the intensity of pleasure: the more physical the source of a pleasure is, the weaker its sensation will be; the more spiritual the source of pleasure, the greater and more intense its sensation will be. This pattern continues to ever-higher levels. Thus, the greatest pleasure that exists in creation is "finding delight in God" (*Mesillas Yesharim*, Ch. 1), which is bestowed upon the souls of people who fulfill mitzvos, for this is the most spiritual pleasure of all.

H. There are four levels of creatures that correspond to the four levels of life

The souls of all physical things are spiritual entities. It is spirituality that gives life to physical matter. Thus the more spiritual something is, the more alive it is. There are four categories of creatures: inanimate objects, vegetation, living creatures, and speaking creatures (humans). Inanimate objects display no signs of life; vegetation has enough life to grow, yet has no inner sense of life — only outsiders can see that it is living; living creatures, such as animals, live and even feel their own life, but it is a low level of life, for their life is coarse, animalistic, and instinctive; humans also grow, live, and feel their life — but in a most sublime way: humans feel that their type of life is special, lofty, and spiritual. They sense that they have a soul, that they are self-determining, and that they are free-willed creatures. And they sense that their life can flow over and inspire others.

I. The fifth level of life

Not all humans, however, are equal. The ultimate human is a person who uses his faculty of free will properly to control his mind and his power of speech; he fulfills his duty in this world, uttering and speaking of God's might. This type of person becomes a "living being," a "speaking, [intelligent] spirit" (*Bereishis* 2:7 and *Targum* there). But there is another type of person; one who is a slave to his animalistic drives. The gap between these two types of humans is like the gap between ordinary living creatures and humans — they are entirely different species! We can therefore say that there is actually a fifth category of existence, to which Jews are expected to belong: "I fashioned this nation for Myself that they might declare My praise" (*Yeshayah* 43:21).

J. God is the ultimate spiritual reality

Now, the most spiritual reality that exists is the Creator, Who is absolutely sanctified and holy. He is completely removed from any trace of physical entity or corporeality, and He is unlike even the most spiritual creatures. He is the source of life and of limitless pleasure (which a person can merit by keeping the mitzvos). By emulating God and walking in His ways, a person can become holy, as is written, "You shall be holy, for I, Hashem your God, am holy" (*Vayikra* 19:2). This is also how a human can cleave to Him and gain infinite pleasure, as is written: "But you, who adhere to Hashem, your God, are all living today" (*Devarim* 4:4). When a person submits his body to his mind's rule, when he comes to know God and His limitless knowledge, and when he comes to see God's ways of goodness and kindness — he then "delights in Hashem" (cf. *Yeshayah* 58:14). The people who are most suited for this relationship with God are the Jews. Of them Rabbi Shimon bar Yochai commented, "You are called, 'Man,' but the nations are not called 'Man,' as is written (*Yechezkel* 34:31), 'You are man'" (*Yevamos* 61a). However, those who do not know God are no better than an animal, as our Sages expounded: "[Avraham said to his lads,] 'Stay here with the donkey' (*Bereishis* 22:5) — "with the one who is like a donkey" (*Yevamos* 62a). The "lads" and Eliezer (Avraham's servant) were like donkeys (see *Rashi* ad loc.), for they — unlike Avraham and Yitzchak — did not see the cloud of God attached to Mount Moriah, they did not even sense God's presence.

K. True pleasure can only be found in the World to Come, but a taste of that spiritual delight can be found in this world as well

The Ramchal (R' Moshe Chaim Luzzato) in his work *Mesillas Yesharim* (Ch. 1) writes: "Now, our Sages of blessed memory have taught us that man was created for the sole [purpose] of [finding] delight in God and enjoying the light of His presence; for this is true delight and the greatest pleasure that can be found. But the place where this delight [can be enjoyed] is actually the World to Come." Although the Ramchal is pointing out that perfect delight — the delight that is appropriate for rewarding a person — can only be experienced in the World to Come, yet we can infer from his words that a minute aspect of this pleasure can be found even in this world. For example, our Sages taught that "Shabbos is a semblance of the World to Come" (see *Berachos* 57a). In fact, by observing Shabbos properly, a person can then go on to attain pleasure from all the mitzvos. Torah scholars, in particular, experience intense pleasure from their attachment to Torah and mitzvos — to the extent possible in this physical world. Thus David HaMelech declared, "One thing I asked of Hashem... would that I dwell in House of Hashem all the days of my life, to behold the sweetness of Hashem" (*Tehillim* 27:4). The plain reading of the verse implies that David was referring to our world. He likewise said, "One day in Your courtyards is better than a thousand [elsewhere]" (ibid. 84:11). I heard from my teacher (who was one of the heads of Yeshivas Chevron), R' Aharon Cohen of blessed memory, that David HaMelech meant that dwelling for even one day in the "courtyards of Hashem," in the place where the *Shechinah* reveals itself, was so pleasurable, so full of life and enjoyment, that experiencing just one day there surpassed the combined experience of a thousand years outside of those "courtyards." Indeed, a taste of supreme spiritual pleasure can be attained in this world!

CHAPTER TWO

Belief in the Creation of the World

A. Adam witnessed the world's creation

Adam, the first human, was created directly by God. Adam was created not as a newborn but as a 20-year-old, with a mature body and an adult mind. Adam's intellect was greater than that of any other creature, as God told the angels, "His wisdom is greater than yours" (*Bereishis Rabbah* 17:4). That is, he possessed full knowledge of all fields of wisdom, including all there is to know of nature as well as all aspects of the Divine wisdom contained in the Torah that was to be given later given by Moshe. Adam was thus witness to God's act of creation!

When Adam was created, he found himself in a world that was fully prepared and "expecting" his arrival, like a guest invited to a banquet. Although he awoke suddenly to this new world, he was not confused about his origin — he was fully aware of the fact that he was the first human, created by God. It was obvious to him that he was created — and not born to someone else — precisely because he was created as an adult and not as a newborn. Adam could not have doubted this fact, for God spoke to him and, in effect, told him that he was created (see *Bereishis* 1:28-31). God then brought all the living creatures of the world before him, so that he would give them names. Using his immense intellect, Adam recognized all the creatures — from the most sublime creatures of Heaven to the lowliest ones on earth — and was deeply aware of the fact that they were all created by one single Creator. Furthermore, he also knew that he was created by that same Creator to be the "crown" and master over the creation. The Sages in the Midrash relate (*Koheles Rabbah* 7:13): "When the Holy One created Adam, He took him around to see all the trees of the Garden of Eden and warned him, 'Look how beautiful and special they are! Know that everything I created was created for you. Make sure you don't ruin and destroy My world.'"

B. Adam sensed that he had a part in the unfolding of creation

In *Bereishis* (2:5) we read: "None of the trees of the field were yet on the land, nor had any of the plants of the field yet sprouted, for Hashem, the All-powerful, had not brought rain upon the earth, [since] there was no man [yet] to work the ground." What is the connection between the presence of a man to work the ground and the bringing of rain? Rashi explains: "[Although] regarding the third day [of creation] it is written, 'the land sprouted vegetation' (ibid. 1:12), this does not mean that they actually came forth above the ground but that they remained at the opening of the ground [i.e. just below the surface] until the sixth day. 'For Hashem... had not yet brought rain' [so the vegetation could not grow]. And why, in fact, had God not caused it to rain? Because 'there was no man [yet] to work the ground' who would appreciate the blessing of having rain. But once Adam was created, and he realized that [rain] was important for the world, he prayed for it and it fell, causing the trees and other vegetation to grow." This event, as well, made it clear to Adam that he was part of an unfolding creation.

With this approach we can perhaps also understand why God created Chavah (Eve, the first woman) only after creating Adam and why He created her using Adam's body: God created Chavah this way to help Adam see that the world was in the midst of being created. Adam did, in fact, recognize this and said, "Never again will a woman be created from a man as this one was created from me — [she is] a bone from my bones and flesh from my flesh!" (*Targum Yonasan ben Uzziel* to *Bereishis* 2:23). Adam thus saw for himself that the world was created by God; that the world was now entrusted to him; that, indeed, it was up to him to realize the potential of the earth — he had to pray for the rain that would bring forth the vegetation; that God placed him in the Garden of Eden; and that God spoke to him on a high level of prophecy, commanding him to work and guard the world.

C. Adam's special level of prophecy

Consider the following passage written by the Ramban:

> *Adam HaRishon, who was created by the Holy One, was the best of the human race in insight and knowledge. God placed him in the best of all places [the Garden of Eden] for his pleasure and benefit... [The Garden of Eden] is the most distinguished place in the lower world because it has the unique characteristic of being [the meeting point between the lower world] and the middle and upper worlds. [This characteristic] makes it the most suitable place on earth for receiving [prophecy]. This is akin to our*

belief that the Land of Israel and Yerushalayim are special places that are extremely suitable for prophecy because of their unique characteristics. This is especially true of the Beis HaMikdash (the Temple), as is written (Bereishis 28:17), "How awe-inspiring is this place. This [place] is none other than the House of God, and this is the gateway to Heaven." [In this verse, Yaakov Avinu] attributed the unexpected prophecy he received to the fact that he was in such a special place. If [this is the case for places that are in the ordinary world] then those who dwell in the Garden of Eden, which is even more suitable [for prophecy, can certainly] discover the most sublime secrets... see [prophetic] visions... and fathom everything a human can possibly know and understand.

— *Toras HaAdam, Shaar HaGemul*

We see, then, that the Creator, may He be blessed, provided Adam with three separate ways by which he could come to know God and gain some insight into Him: (a) He was allowed to see for himself some of the acts of creation; (b) he was given unparalleled wisdom and insight into the nature of the world; and (c) he was prophetically told by God that he was created — and there is no clarity as great as the clarity gained by prophecy. Furthermore, the conditions of Adam's life — his personal perfection and his position in the Garden of Eden — made him uniquely suited to prophecy and understanding. And, indeed, Adam did come to see and know that it was God Who created the world.

D. This knowledge was passed on to the future generations

Adam passed on his knowledge of the creation to his son — and spiritual heir — Shes. Like his father, Shes also possessed superb characteristics and faculties, as the Torah testifies, "He then fathered [a son] resembling him [and] with his form, and named him Shes" (*Bereishis* 5:3). Included in the knowledge transmitted to Shes was the fact that the world was created ex nihilo — out of nonexistence, by God — and the wisdom that God had given to Adam. This knowledge was then passed on from generation to generation: Shes passed it to Chanoch, Chanoch to Mesushelach, Mesushelach to Noach, Noach to Shem, Shem to Ever, Shem together with Ever passed it on to Avraham and his descendants (Yitzchak and Yaakov). In addition, those early generations lived very long lives, so that it was possible to learn this knowledge from much earlier generations directly: "Mesushelach [saw] Adam HaRishon and served him for 243 years, Shem saw Mesushelach and served him for 48 years, Yaakov saw Shem and served him for 80 years, and Amram saw Yaakov" (*Shalsheles HaKabbalah*).

E. The Ramban's outline of this tradition

The Torah recounts [the lineage of the world's nations] because it wanted to show that Avraham descended from Shem [and therefore why he received the Land of Israel].... Furthermore, the [Rambam] in Moreh HaNevuchim (III:50) writes that this [account] verifies to those who hear [of it] the fact that the world was created new. This is quite true, for our forefather Avraham directed his sons and his household after him (see Bereishis 18:19) and attested the existence of Noach and his children who saw the Flood and were in the Ark. Thus, he was a witness to a witness to the Flood, and a fourth generation witness to the creation of the world (Noach saw his father [Lemech], and [Lemech] saw Adam HaRishon). [That chain of witnesses continued, for] Yitzchak and Yaakov saw Shem, who was a direct witness to the Flood. Then Yaakov recounted this to those who went down to Egypt, as well as to Pharaoh and the rest of that generation. [Even now,] there are people in every generation [who have a tradition of these events] from their forebears — going back four, and sometimes five, generations.

— Ramban, Commentary to Bereishis 10:5

That there was no room for doubt about the creation of the world — at least for as long as Adam was alive — we see from another passage in the *Ramban* (Commentary to 2:3): "The six days of creation correspond to [the 6,000 years] that the world will exist.... The creation of the first day was light, which corresponds to the [expected thousand] years of Adam, who was the light of the world, and who recognized his Creator. It could very well be that Enosh did not commit idolatry until Adam HaRishon passed away [and if so the light remained intact throughout the entire thousand years]." Apparently, the mistake of idolatry was unthinkable, even to Enosh, as long as the "light" that witnessed the creation of the world was alive, for Adam — who was so perfectly created by God — was himself testimony to the creation of the world.

F. Another proof of Adam's greatness

In the book of *Devarim* (4:32) we read: "Ask now about earlier times that were before you, from the day that God created man on earth, and [ask every being that exists] from one end of the heavens to the other: Was there ever [at any other time anything] like this great thing, or was something like it ever heard of?" The Talmud comments on this verse:

> *Said Rabbi Elazar: "[At first] Adam HaRishon extended from the earth until heaven, as is written, 'from the day that God created man on earth ... [to the end of the heavens],' but once he degenerated, the Holy One placed His hand on him and reduced him, as is written (Tehillim 139:5), 'Back and front You have restricted me, and You have laid Your hand upon me.'" [For a similar idea presented by Rav Yehudah in the name of Rav, see the Talmud there.]*
>
> — *Chagigah 12a*

G. If not for sin, Adam could have forever inspired others to believe in God

Elsewhere in the Talmud, we are shown yet another aspect of Adam's greatness:

> *R' Bana'eh used to mark burial caves [to protect items from becoming ritually impure] .... When he reached the cave of Adam HaRishon a bas kol (a voice from Heaven) came out and said, "Though you saw the resemblance of My image [i.e. Yaakov], do not gaze at My image itself [i.e. Adam, of whom it is written (Bereishis 1:27), 'He created him with God's form' — Rashbam]." Said R' Bana'eh: "I looked at Adam's two heels, and they were like the disks of two suns. An ordinary person compared to Sarah was like a monkey next to a human; Sarah compared to Chavah was like a monkey next to a human; and Chavah compared to Adam was like a monkey next to a human."*
>
> — *Bava Basra 58a*

Since Adam HaRishon was such a remarkable person, we can be certain that if not for his and his children's sins, which brought darkness and confusion into the world (and which led to the falsehood of idolatry in the days of Enosh), there would have been enough Godly wisdom in Adam to sustain the world's belief in God — forever!

CHAPTER THREE

The Development of Idolatry

A. The Rambam's account of the origins of idol worship

The Rambam in the first chapter of *Hilchos Avodas Kochavim* (The Laws of Idolatry) elaborates on the origins of idolatry, how people arrived at that error, and how the erroneous belief spread. Here we quote the first two paragraphs verbatim, so that we can hear the full fire of the Rambam's description:

> *In the days of Enosh, people arrived at a major and foolish error. The scholars of that generation, including Enosh, were among the mistaken ones. What was their error? They said: Since God created the planets and the constellations to govern the world, and He placed them in the sky to give them*

honor, and they are His attendants, then it is only fitting that we, too, praise, exalt, and honor them. They believed that the Almighty Himself, may He be blessed, wanted them to exalt and honor the ones whom He honored. [In their thinking,] this is like a king who wants respect shown to his ministers — by doing so, it is really the king who is being honored. Once this thought entered their hearts, they began building temples to the stars and offering sacrifices to them. They verbally praised and exalted them and bowed before them. All this was — in their skewed thought — to fulfill the will of the Creator. At first, this was the central element of idolatry [which was technically star-worship] — to those who understood its essence and as those who worshiped them professed — but they did not claim that the star was God. Thus, the prophet Yirmiyah says (10:7-8), "Who would not fear You, O King of the nations? For [kingship] befits You; for among all the wise men of the nations and in all their kingdoms [it is known that] there is none like You. They are uniformly foolish and stupid, the vain [idols] for which they are punished; it is [but] wood." That is, they all knew that You are the only One, but their foolish mistake was that they thought that this folly was actually Your will.

— Rambam, Avodas Kochavim 1:1

B. Subsequent mistakes of the nations

In the next paragraph, the Rambam describes the second step in the development of idolatry:

After many days, false prophets emerged who claimed that God commanded that they worship a certain star (or all of the stars): "[You are] to offer sacrifices and wine libations to it, build a temple to it, and make an image of it in order to bow before it — everyone: men, women, and children." They then instructed the people to fashion a certain shape, which they had made up in their heart, and told them, "This is the image of the such-and-such star," which they had been told in their "prophecy." Thus, they began making graven images everywhere: in the temples, beneath the trees, on the mountains, and on the hilltops. [These "prophets"] would gather together and bow to them while telling the masses that "this particular image bestows good or does harm, so serve it properly and fear it." Or the priests would tell them, "By doing this service you will multiply and be successful. Do such-and-such, but do not do this-and-that." More liars then presented themselves and claimed that the star, the planet, or the angel itself spoke with them, and told them, "Serve me in such-and-such a way. Do this and don't do that!" These [lies] finally spread throughout the world, [demanding of the masses] to serve the images in ever stranger ways, to sacrifice to them, and to bow to them. Eventually, the glorified and fearful Name [of God] was forgotten entirely .... It thus came about that the masses, the women, and the children knew nothing but the images made of wood and stone and the stone temples [that they had built]. For this is how they were educated from their youth — to bow to them, to serve them, and to swear by their names. Even the wise men among them, such as the priests, assumed that there is no higher power other than the planets and the constellations (of which they had made images). But there was no one who recognized [God] and knew of Him save a few individuals, such as Chanoch, Mesushelach, Noach, Shem, and Ever. The world continued in this manner until the "pillar of the world" was born: our forefather Avraham.

— Rambam, Avodas Kochavim 1:2

C. There are three types of idolaters

The Ramban (Nachmanides), in his commentary to the verse, "You must not have any gods of others as long as I exist" (*Shemos* 20:3), offers a slightly different description of how idolatry developed:

There were three types of idolatry.

The first type of idolatry was when people began worshiping the angels, which are purely intelligent beings [i.e. they have no physical body]. Since some of them are known to possess dominion over the nations... [people] thought that the angels themselves have the power to bestow good or inflict bad, so each [nation] served its own officer-angel....

The second type of idolaters developed when people turned to worship the visible hosts of the sky; some served the sun or the moon while others worshiped one of the constellations of the zodiac, for each nation knew which was their constellation. [The people who worshiped the zodiac] believed that by worshiping their constellation, they would give it more strength, which, in turn, would benefit them.... These are the people who began making the myriad images of the statues, asherah-trees, and sun gods; for they were making the images of the constellations [as they appeared during] the hours [they believed] to have power... when they would [supposedly] give the people power and success.... This probably began in the generation of the Dispersion, when God scattered the [people] to the various countries and the stars and constellations [began] ruling over them as separate [nations].... Now, each group had its own set of false prophets who — using the techniques of sorcery and divination — would predict some of the future events that were to come upon [their nation].

— Ramban, Commentary to Shemos 20:3

D. Why did people start worshiping humans?

After describing the second type of idolaters, the Ramban explains that the practice of worshiping a human is actually an extension of this second type:

From this [second] type of worship, some of them went on to idolize people, for when they saw that an individual had great dominion over others and his mazal (constellation) was ascending in an extraordinary way — such as Nevuchadnezzar's ascent — the people of that person's country thought that by accepting upon themselves to worship him and by dedicating themselves to him, their mazal will also rise, along with his mazal. That individual, as well, believed that when the [people's] thoughts are attached to his, he would become even more successful — by the power of their focused souls. This is what Pharaoh thought, as our Sages taught. This is also what Sancheriv thought, of whose thoughts it is written (Yeshayah 14:14), "I will ascend over the tops of the clouds; I will liken myself to the Most High!" Chiram and his friends, as well, made themselves into gods (see Chullin 89a). These people were wicked, not total fools [because they knew about the mazalos; yet they were wrong because they thought that being worshiped would have a real effect on their success. Still, they were more wicked than foolish because they denied the fact that God ultimately controls the mazalos].

E. Differences and similarities between the Rambam and Ramban concerning the motives of the early idolaters

The Ramban's suggestion that idol worship "probably began in the generation of the Dispersion" clearly refers to the second type of idolatry — the worship of stars and constellations — since the Ramban only wrote this in his discussion of the second type. But the first type of idolatry — the worship of angels — began much earlier, primarily in the generation of Enosh (that is, eight generations earlier), as the Rambam (Maimonides) quoted above makes clear and as the Ramban (Nachmanides) himself wrote in his commentary to *Shemos* (13:16): "From the time idolatry began in the days of Enosh, [people's] opinions in matters of faith became confused." It would seem, then, that there is no disagreement between the Rambam and the Ramban concerning the question of when idolatry began. Nevertheless, there does seem to be two differences between them: (a) The Rambam maintains that the first stage of idolatry consisted mainly of worshiping stars and constellations (he only mentions "the angel" and "angels" in paragraph two and in the beginning of Chapter Two), while the Ramban maintains that the first stage consisted only of worshiping angels. (b) In describing the motives of the first idolaters, the Rambam writes that their mistake was to "honor the servants of God," while the Ramban writes that "they thought they had the power to do good or harm." However, we know from other sources in the Ramban's writings that he did agree with the Rambam on this last point. For example, in his commentary to *Shemos* 22:19, on the verse, "He who sacrifices to idols shall be put to death; only to Hashem alone [may one sacrifice]," he writes: "It says, 'Only to Hashem alone [may one sacrifice],' because those who worship to His angels thought that they were doing [God's] will, that [the angels] were intermediaries to gain goodwill from Him; [in their minds,] it was as though they were sacrificing to Him and to His attendants. The verse, therefore, [emphasizes] 'only to Hashem alone.'" And, again, in his commentary (ibid. 23:25) the Ramban writes like the Rambam: "[Those who worship angels most certainly] think that they will receive extra blessing by serving the angels because they are honoring the servants of the great God."

F. The third type of idolatry

The Ramban continues:

> *[The second type continued with] the third type of idolatry: The people turned to worshiping sheidim (demons), which are spirits, as I will God-willing explain. [The reason they turned to them was] because some of them are appointed over the nations and are the masters over those countries — to harm their enemies and their feeble ones. This is known from the science of necromancy, as well as from our Sages. About this [group] the verse says (Devarim 32:17), "They sacrificed to demons that have no purpose, gods that*

they did not [previously] know; new [idols] that were [only] recently [worshiped], of which your fathers had no fear." The verse mocks them for sacrificing to demons that are not really gods at all — they are not even like angels that are at least known as "gods"; rather, these [creatures] are "gods that they did not know" — they are not known to have any authority or power — and they are "new" in that [the people] had only recently learned to [worship them] from the Egyptians who practice witchcraft. [The verse points out that] even their [idolatrous] ancestors, such as Terach and Nimrod, never feared them. Because of this type, the verse warns (Vayikra 17:7), "And [the Children of Israel] shall no longer sacrifice their sacrifices to the se'eerim (demons) after whom they stray."

— Ramban, Commentary to Shemos 20:3

To complete our description of the third type of idolaters, we conclude with the Ramban's commentary to *Vayikra*:

> *"To the se'eerim" — to the sheidim (demons)... this is the opinion of Rashi. Rabbi Avraham [Ibn Ezra] said, "Demons are called [se'eerim] because they cause people who see them to make their hair [se'ar] stand on end [out of fear]. [More] likely, they are called this because lunatics see them in the form of goats (se'eerim). The words 'no longer' imply that this is what the Jews did practice in Egypt. 'After whom they stray' — because anyone who believes in them and seeks them out, strays from the glorified and awesome God."*
>
> *— Ramban, Commentary to Vayikra 17:7*

CHAPTER FOUR

Faith in One God and the Origins of the Jewish People

A. Our forefather Avraham realized that there is only One God

The world had all but forgotten God, as described in the previous chapter, yet one person restored the awareness of God to the world. That person was Avraham Avinu.

Let us turn again to the Rambam for a description of Avraham's beginnings and how the Jewish people developed from him:

> *Once this mighty one [Avraham] was weaned, he began pondering [about the world] — though he was still a*

child. He started thinking day and night, and he wondered: How is it possible for this orb [Earth] to operate continuously without anyone operating it? Who makes it turn? It cannot possibly spin by itself!

He had no one to teach him and no one who could inform him. On the contrary, he was deeply set in Ur Kasdim, among foolish idol worshipers. [In his day,] everybody worshiped idols and stars — including his father and mother — and he, too, worshiped along with the rest. Yet his heart continued to rove until he came upon the path of Truth and the route of Justice. Thus, with his keen insight, he realized that there exists a single God, that it is He who created everything and Who operates the planet, and that no other god exists. It was obvious to him that the entire world was mistaken, and that the root of their error was their [extensive] worship of stars and graven images, until they forgot the truth [about God].

[Avraham's awareness of God began developing when he was 3 years old.] By the time he was 40, he [fully] recognized his Creator. With this clear awareness, he began debating with the people of Ur Kasdim [about their belief] and responding to their questions. He told them that "the path you are on is not the path of truth." He broke their idols. In this way, he began informing the people that the only One to Whom it is proper to worship is the God of the universe; only to Him is it proper to bow, to sacrifice, and to pour libations — so that all people who are yet to come will recognize Him. And [he explained to the people] that it is proper to destroy and demolish all the graven images so that other people… do not err in them.

But when he managed to prove them wrong, the king decided to have him killed. Miraculously, he succeeded in escaping, and he set out to Charan. [There, too,] he began teaching and proclaiming to the whole world that the universe has only one single God and that it is proper to serve [only] Him. In his travels, he continued publicizing

[God's existence], while gathering [followers] from every city and country [on his path]. He continued in this manner until he reached the land of Canaan. [There, too,] he continued calling out, as is written (Bereishis 21:33): "And there he proclaimed the Name of Hashem, God of the Universe." When people congregated before him and asked him about his assertions, he would inspire each person individually — in accord with that person's faculties — until he succeeded in directing [many individuals] toward the path of truth. Eventually, tens of thousands of people gathered to him. These are "the people of Avraham's household" [mentioned in ibid. 17:23]. In their hearts, he planted the great principle [of God's existence and unity], and he wrote books for them. Later, he passed on this information to his son Yitzchak, who then set out to teach and exhort [others]. Yitzchak, in turn, instructed Yaakov and appointed him as a teacher. [So Yaakov then] settled down to teach and encourage all those who accompanied him. Yaakov taught all his sons, but separated Levi and appointed him as the leader. He also installed him in a yeshivah, to teach [others about] the way of Hashem [and about] Avraham's precepts. Levi charged his children to make sure that they always have somebody appointed [to teach] in order to ensure that the lessons would never be forgotten. [This pattern] continued and intensified among the children of Yaakov and among those who accompanied them; and thus a nation who knew of God was formed in the world.

But after the Jews had been in Egypt for many days, they learned to act like [the Egyptians] and worship stars like them. The only exception was the tribe of Levi who remained faithful to the instructions of the Fathers, for the tribe of Levi never worshiped idols. At any moment the root that Avraham planted was about to be uprooted, and the children of Yaakov were about to [completely] revert to the world's errors and wayward behavior. Yet because of

God's love for us and because He kept the oath that He swore to our forefather Avraham (see Devarim 7:8), He prepared and sent Moshe Rabbeinu, the master of all the prophets, [to save them]. Once Moshe Rabbeinu received prophecy and God chose Israel as His portion, He crowned them with commandments and told them how they are to serve Him and what is the penalty for those who commit idolatry.

— Rambam, Avodas Kochavim 1:3

B. God redeemed the Jews in Egypt because He loves the Jewish people

A simple reading of the Rambam may give us the impression that had the Jews not committed idolatry in Egypt — and thus there would have been no danger to the principles of true faith — it would not have been necessary to redeem them, or, for that matter, give them the Torah. But that is not so, for even if they would have heeded Avraham's instructions, their good deeds would have remained voluntary, lacking Divine command. This is not an ideal state because of the halachic principle, "Greater is one who does when commanded than one who does without being commanded" (*Kiddushin* 31a). The only way they could have been commanded by God was by receiving the Torah. Moreover, we know that the entire universe was held in a state of abeyance, waiting for the sixth day — that is, the sixth day of Sivan, which was destined to be the day when the Torah would be given to Israel (see *Rashi* to *Bereishis* 1:31). Too much was dependent on the giving of the Torah for it not to be given. For these reasons we must conclude that the Exodus from Egypt and the giving of the Torah were certainly essential events for the Jews. But perhaps the Rambam meant only to imply that by following the idolatry of Egypt the Jews almost jeopardized their Exodus, and they ran the risk of not getting out even at the predetermined time to leave. But had they been good all along, they certainly would have left Egypt. This approach would match the Ramban's opinion, as he writes in his commentary to *Shemos* (2:25): "'God saw the Children of Israel['s situation]....' Although the decreed time had been completed, they were not worthy of being redeemed, as is explicitly stated by [the prophet] Yechezkel (see *Yechezkel* 20:8). But because of their cry, [God] compassionately accepted their prayer." A careful reading of the Rambam, in fact, shows the same point: "At any moment the root that Avraham planted was about to be uprooted," because "the children of Yaakov were about to [completely] revert to the world's errors and wayward behavior." Their sins should have caused them to remain in Egypt past the predetermined time of redemption, yet "because of God's love for us" He did not leave them there.

But, we may wonder, if the Jews in Egypt were really wicked, how could God love them? The answer might lie in the Ramban's remarks on the verse, "Do not say to yourself as follows, 'Because of my righteousness, Hashem brought me [here] to take possession of this land'.... It is not because of your righteousness... but in order to fulfill the word that Hashem promised to your forefathers, Avraham, Yitzchak and Yaakov" (*Devarim* 9:4-5):

> *One could ask: Does it not say earlier (Devarim 7:8), "Out of Hashem's love for you, [and because He kept the oath that He swore to your forefathers, Hashem took you out... from the house of slavery...]"; clearly, they are beloved to [the One] Above, and since God only loves those who are good — for He detests the wicked and those who enjoy stealing (see Yeshayah 1:14) — then they must have been righteous enough to take possession of the land?! [How, then, could our verse say that they did not inherit the land "because of your righteousness"?] The answer is: There [the Torah] was referring to the Jewish people as a whole, but here it was giving rebuke to that particular generation who were rebellious against God [(as is clear from verse 9:7)].*
>
> — *Ramban, Commentary to Devarim 9:4-5*

We can apply the Ramban's distinction regarding inheriting the land to the Exodus from Egypt: True, the particular generation of Jews who lived in Egypt were sinful — as the verse in *Yechezkel* (20:8) states — but the Jewish people as a whole are always beloved before God. Accordingly, the verse in *Devarim* (7:8) is referring to the love of the Jewish people in its entirety: "Out of Hashem's love for you, and because He kept the oath that He swore to your forefathers, Hashem took you out with mighty force and redeemed you from the house of slavery, from the clutches of Pharaoh, king of Egypt." If you think about it, you will see that when the Rambam writes that we were redeemed "because of God's love for us," he was referring to this verse — and was making the same point: God redeemed the Jews in Egypt — thought they were not worthy — because he loves "us" — the Jewish people as a whole. Even if an entire generation sins, it does not mean that the entire Jewish people have sinned, because "the Jewish people" is a composite of all the generations — and, as such, they can never fail! Why does He love us? Because, as a whole, we have never failed Him. And where does this strength come from? From the power of Avraham, as the Rambam concludes.

CHAPTER FIVE

Divine Providence

A. God created several universes and conducts them all

A fundamental Torah belief is that God operates and conducts the world. Of particular importance is the belief that God extends specific providence (*hashgachah pratis*) over his nation, Israel. As the Rishonim, the Earlier Rabbis, taught, this belief is the foundation of the entire Torah.

God created several universes. For this discussion, we will focus on three: *Beriah*/Creation, *Yetzirah*/Formation, and *Asiyah*/Action. The Rishonim sometimes used a different set of names when they discussed these universes; they are: the "Upper world," the "Middle world," and the "Lower world." The Upper universe encompasses the angels — the glorious servants of God; these are creatures who are purely conceptual (i.e. they have no "bodies" whatsoever). The Middle universe contains the heavenly bodies such as the planets and the stars. And the Lower universe contains planet Earth.

B. The universes are influenced in descending order

God both created and sustains these universes with His "speech." Thus it is written (*Tehillim* 33:6), "By the word of Hashem the heavens were made," and it is written (ibid.119:89), "Forever, Hashem, Your word stands firm in heaven." These universes are connected in descending order: each one acts as a "soul," or "root," for the universe below it. The higher the universe, the more spiritual it is. We can therefore say that God's spiritual influence unfolds and descends from one universe to the next. The sequence of this influence is as follows: When God's influence reaches the angels, in the universe of *Beriah*/Creation, the angels become conduits to the planets and constellations, thereby becoming the soul for the *Yetzirah*/Formation universe; then, in turn, the planets and constellations become the soul for the universe of *Asiyah*/Action — planet Earth. However, as R' Avraham Ibn Ezra clarifies, this does not mean that God does not directly interact with the lower universes:

> *[God] alone remains unchanging; there is nothing else eternal, nor anyone like Him "Who is enthroned from days of old, Selah" (Tehillim 55:20). He supports the Upper world with His might; the Middle world with His Name and [with] His holy angels who are in the Upper world; and He supports our Lower universe with the power of the Name and with the power of the two higher worlds.*
>
> *— Ibn Ezra, Commentary to Shemos 20:1*

C. Who is governed by mazal?

The inhabitants of Earth are therefore said to be governed by mazal, the zodiac, but, more accurately, they are really directed through the higher universes. We can gain a better understanding of this concept from the Ramban:

> *"The land became defiled and I exacted retribution on it for its transgressions, so the land spewed out [its inhabitants]" (Vayikra 18:25). [The Torah] is very strict when it comes to incest because the land becomes defiled as a result, and it cannot tolerate those souls that commit [such acts]. Note that incest is a prohibition of the body and is not actually dependent on the Land [of Israel, so why does it make any difference where it is committed?] The key to the matter lies in the following verse (Devarim 32:8-9), "When the Most High gave nations their heritage and dispersed mankind, He set the borders of nations.... For Hashem's portion is His people...." [God] created everything and then [arranged the world in a way] that gave the control of lower [beings] to higher ones. [For example,] He appointed specific planets and constellations to govern each one of the nations in their own country — as is well known in astrology. Thus it is written, "[When you raise your eyes to the sky, and see the sun, moon, stars and other heavenly bodies, do not bow down to them or worship them.] It was to all the other nations under the heavens that Hashem, your God, has assigned them" (ibid. 4:19). For He assigned stars in the sky for all of them, and, above them, the Most High assigned His angels to be officers over them — as in the verse, "But the officer-angel of the Persian kingdom stood opposed to me..." (Daniel 10:13) and in the verse, "behold — the officer-angel of Greece approaches" (ibid. v. 20). [These angels] are also known as "kings" as is written, "For I had remained there alone beside the kings of Persia" (ibid. v. 13).*
>
> *— Ramban, Commentary to Vayikra 18:25*

This system of mazalos and angels is not independent of God nor is it universal, as the Ramban continues:

> *While Hashem is, [of course,] the God of all powers that exist and is the Lord over all lords,*[1] *still, the land of Israel [is unique]. As the center of the world, it is the "heritage of Hashem" (cf. I Shmuel 26:19); it is designated to His Name alone: He did not assign any of the angels to it to be its chief, governor or officer. [Instead,] He gave it as a heritage to His nation who proclaim His unity, the seed of those who loved Him. It is thus written, "You alone will be a special treasure for Me, more than all the nations, [even though] all the earth is Mine" (Shemos 19:5). It is also written, "You will be a people for Me and I will be a God for you" (Yirmiyah 11:4) — you will not be subject to any other power [such as angels or stars as are the nations].*
>
> *— Ramban, Commentary to Vayikra 18:25*

D. The function of mazalos in the course of history

The mazal of a nation governs not only how much sustenance that nation will receive but also the course of its history. Consequently, whatever happens to a nation depends on the position of its constellation, which is determined by its officer-

1. See *Devarim* 10:17. The word *elohim,* meaning "all powers," used to describe the angels should not be confused with the Name of God, *Elokim.* The reason angels are called *elohim* is because the word is related to the word *el,* which simply means powerful. It is their powerful role that gives them their name. Whatever power they have, though, is handed to them by God, as they have no independent source of strength or will. Angels cannot determine, add, or subtract any sustenance set for the world; an angel is more like a pipe than a fountain. Whatever is effected by them is only in accord with God's will. This is why the Hebrew word for an angel is *malach,* which means, a messenger — just like a prophet is sometimes called a *malach,* as in: "He sent a messenger who took us out of Egypt" (*Bamidbar* 20:16), referring to Moshe Rabbeinu; and as in: "And [the prophet] Chaggai, the agent (*malach*) of Hashem... spoke to the people" (*Chaggai* 1:13). Similarly, although the stars in the zodiac are called lords and rulers — as in, "God made... the great luminary to rule the day, and the lesser luminary to rule the night" (*Bereishis* 1:16) — the true source of their power is God, Whose will alone activates everything.

angel with whatever power God decreed it would have. An illustration of this concept can be found in the Ramban, in the name of *Pirkei D'Rabi Eliezer*:[2]

> *[Yaakov's vision of the ladder] was similar to [the incident of the Covenant] Between the Halves experienced by Avraham [in that it was a vision of future events] where He showed him the dominion of the four exiles, including their ascent and descent. This is the significance of the "angels of God" (Bereishis 28:12) because they are like [the angels] mentioned in [the book of] Daniel, "the officer-angel of the Persian kingdom" (Daniel 10:13)... "the officer-angel of Greece approaches" (ibid. v. 20).... [Our Sages] said: The Holy One showed him the four kingdoms [that were destined to rule the world] — both their rule and their demise. He showed him the angel appointed over Babylon climb 70 rungs and then come back down [alluding to the 70 years of Jewish exile in the Babylonian empire]; he saw the officer-angel of Media climb 52 rungs and come back down; then Greece climbing 180 rungs....*
>
> — *Ramban, Commentary to Bereishis 28:12*

E. An individual's mazal

Likewise, every individual has his own mazal, set by the position of the zodiac at the time of the person's formation — all in accord with God's decree.[3] Rabbi Chanina bar Pappa in Gemara *Niddah* (16b) expounded: "The angel that is appointed over conception is called *Lelah.* It takes a drop and presents it before the Holy One, and says, 'Master of the Universe! This drop — what will become of it? Will it be mighty or weak? Wise or foolish? Wealthy or poor...?'" Thus the circumstances of life are determined before a person is even born. In the same Gemara, Rabbi Chanina taught:

---

2. This passage is unfortunately missing in our editions of the *Pirkei D'Rabi Eliezer.*

3. In this regard, the Jewish view of the role of the zodiac differs greatly from the view held by all other nations, for we believe that the zodiac itself is really a manifestation of God's decree. Furthermore, we believe that one's constellation only governs the circumstances of that person's life but not how he will use or react to those circumstances. A person's actions are not predetermined. -ed.

"Everything is in the hands of Heaven except for the fear of Heaven." As *Tosafos* there (s.v. *Hakol bidei Shamayim*) demonstrates, this rule is true both concerning one's character traits as well as the incidents and events the person will encounter in life.

F. "Everything depends on mazal"

But mazal is not limited to humans — it extends to all creatures and types of vegetation, as the Ramban writes:

> *Plants and all the living creatures need primary forces [i.e. sources of life in a higher realm] for them to grow.... Our Sages have said (Bereishis Rabbah 10:6): "There isn't a single blade of grass down below that does not have a mazal in heaven who hits it and tells it, 'Grow!' Thus it is written (Iyov 38:33), 'Do you know the laws of heaven; did you place its rule [mishtaro] upon the land?' [Did you appoint an officer (shoter) for the land?]"*
>
> — *Ramban, Commentary to Bereishis 2:8*

Indeed, "Everything depends on mazal" (*Zohar, Nasso*, 134)!

G. There are individuals who merit special supervision

God, however, conducts the world with more than just one system: Almost everything that exists, including ordinary people, is governed with a general system of God's supervision via the forces of heaven; but individuals who recognize, serve, and become attached to God are governed by Him in a direct manner. Such individuals merit God's special supervision and protection, and He exempts them from the normal constraints of nature — those laws that He had ordained for the world.[4] In the words of the Ibn Ezra:

> *I will now reveal to you part of the secret of "E-l Sh-dai": We know that God created the worlds mentioned earlier,*

4. This is related to the topic of *hashgachah pratis*, "specific Divine providence," which will be discussed in greater detail in Chapters Eight and Nine.

including the lower world. The lower world receives the energy it needs for all its details from the middle world — in consonance with the upper system [of the constellations]. But since the soul of a human is higher than the middle world, if a person was wise and recognized God's deeds — both those that He does directly and those that He does through an intermediary — and desisted from the desires of the lower level, and instead devoted himself to "the glorious Name," then even if there had been a decree set at the time of his conception that an evil event will befall him on a certain day, the Name that he attached himself to will bring about the circumstances that will save him from the calamity. If, based on his constellation, this [righteous] person should have been sterile, God will correct his ability to have children — and he will have children. This is why God told Avraham (Nedarim 32a), "Leave your constellation!" (this is probably also the reason why "there is no mazal for Israel" [ibid. and Shabbos 152a])....

God therefore told Avraham, "I am the All-sufficing God [Ani E-l Sh-dai] (Bereishis 15:1) — before telling him "I will make you exceedingly numerous" (ibid. v. 2) — because it means "[I can give you children despite your mazal because] I am the One Who overpowers the upper systems." The system of nature, in this case, is not shattered, it is just manipulated for the person who attached himself to [God], such that he is assured that [God] will bring about the good though it was not originally in his array. Thus Yaakov said (ibid. 48:16), "the angel who delivers me from all the evil" that was destined to come upon me. This is the secret of the entire Torah!

— Ibn Ezra, Commentary to Shemos 6:3

CHAPTER SIX

The Exodus From Egypt

A. The Exodus is a central source of faith in God

An essential idea that emerges from many verses of the Torah and from the teachings of the Rabbis is that the Exodus from Egypt is the main source for faith in God and for many other aspects of Torah faith.[1] This explains why the Torah mentions the Exodus more than any other event. In fact, the *Zohar* (*Yisro* 85b) writes that the Torah

1. This is clear from many verses throughout the Torah. See, for example the book of *Shemos* (12:14, 17, 27; 13:3, 8-9, 14-16) and the book of *Devarim* (5:15): "You shall remember that you were once a slave in the land of Egypt, but Hashem, your God, brought you out from there with mighty force and extended power, and therefore Hashem, your God, has commanded you to observe the Shabbos day." See also *Devarim* 6:21.

refers to the Exodus no less than fifty times. The author of *Sefer HaChinuch* elaborates on this idea:

> *[The twenty-first mitzvah is] to recount, on the evening of the fifteenth of Nissan, the departure from Egypt ... so that one should remember the miracles and the events that occurred for our forefathers in [connection with] the Exodus from Egypt; and how God, may He be blessed, took revenge upon the [Egyptians] for us ....*
>
> *At the root of this precept lies what was written above about the Pesach offering (Mitzvah §18). We need not wonder why we have received so many precepts — both positive and negative — for the [purpose of remembering the Exodus], as it is a great foundation and mighty pillar of our Torah and of our faith. For this reason, as well, we frequently say in our blessings and our prayers, "a commemoration of the departure from Egypt." [For the Exodus] was a full indication and proof that the world was created out of nonexistence, and that there is a preexistent God Who possesses will and power; that it is He Who gives all created things their being; and that it is in His power to change them as He wishes, at any particular time — [just] as He did in Egypt. [For at that time] He altered the world's nature for our sake, and made great and mighty signs for us — miracles that have never been done before. Surely this must silence anyone who would deny the creation of the world out of nonexistence, while it affirms faith in God's knowledge [of the world], and that His watchful control and power extends to all groups and individuals.*
>
> — *Sefer HaChinuch §21*

B. The Mitzvah of tefillin is a primary example of this concept

These words of the *Sefer HaChinuch* echo the Ramban's discussion of the lessons of the mitzvah of *tefillin.* This passage of the Ramban is found in his commentary to *Sefer Shemos*, at the end of *Parshas Bo*:

> *"'Uletotafos' between your eyes" (Shemos 13:16); there is no other word directly related to this word, [uletotafos]. Linguists, however, associated it with the expressions: "proclaim (v'hateif) southward" (Yechezkel 21:2); "My speech would drip (titof) upon them" (Iyov 29:22). This figurative [word for speaking] is a borrowed term from [the verse]: "The mountains will drip (v'hiteefu) juice" (Amos 9:13). Thus [our verse] is saying that you should make the Exodus from Egypt a sign upon your hand, and [make it] "a source of speech between your eyes" that will "flow like dew" upon those who hear it (see Devarim 32:2). Our Rabbis, however, call ornaments that lie upon the head totafos [accordingly, the verse is saying, "make this... an ornament between your eyes]. And since it was the Rabbis [of the Talmud] who were the [true Hebrew] linguists, as they spoke the language and knew it best, it is from them that we should accept [the explanation of the word uletotafos].*
>
> *Note that the Torah says totafos [in the plural] and not totefes [in the singular] because there are several compartments in tefillin. This is in accord with the tradition passed down to us from our holy fathers who saw the prophets and the elders, who had this tradition going back to our teacher, Moshe.*
>
> *The fundamental element of this commandment is that we place the script of the Exodus from Egypt upon the hand and upon the head, corresponding to the heart and the brain — the two pivots of thought. Thus we are to inscribe [on parchment] the [Torah] sections of Kadesh ("Sanctify for Me" [Shemos 13:1-10]), and V'hayah ki yeviacha ("It will be when Hashem brings you" [ibid. vs.11-16]), and then enclose them in the tefillin [in order to fulfill] this commandment where we were charged to make the Exodus from Egypt "an ornament between our*

eyes." [We are also to inscribe and enclose in the tefillin the sections of] Shema ("Hear O Israel" [Devarim 6:4-9]) and V'hayah im shamo'a ("This will be, if you constantly heed My commandments" [ibid. 11:13-21]) because we are also charged to have the commandments [of the Torah] made into ornaments between our eyes, as is written: "These things that I am commanding you today shall be [impressed] upon you heart" (ibid. 6:6), [and it is written,] "You shall tie them upon your hand, and they shall be as ornaments (totafos) between your eyes" (ibid. v. 8). The reason why we also inscribe these two sections — [Shema and V'hayah im shamo'a] — as ornaments [even though the Exodus is not mentioned in them] is that they contain the commandment of the Unity of God, the obligation to remember all the commandments, the principle of reward and punishment [for keeping or disobeying the commandments], and the entire root of faith.

[The Torah] says of the arm tefillin, "And it shall remain as a sign for you on your hand" (Shemos 13:9); this refers to the left arm, opposite the heart, as the Rabbis explained (Menachos 36b)....

Then [the verse] says, "[And it shall remain]... as a reminder between your eyes," meaning that we are to lay them at the place of memory, which is between the eyes, at the beginning of the brain. It is the place where memory begins and where images [of persons and events] are stored after they have passed away from us. This "ornament" encircles around the whole head with its straps, while the loop rests directly over the base of the brain which guards the memory.

— Ramban, Commentary to Shemos 13:16

The Ramban is pointing out that (a) the remembrance of the Exodus should be as full and complete as possible; (b) this can be accomplished by making full use of one's thought process and power of memory; and (c) external actions influence internal awareness. All this, as we will soon discuss, was included in God's decree and command.

c. Many of the mitzvos are intended to be reminders of God's providence

The Ramban continues:

> *I will now tell you a general principle that explains the rationale behind many of the commandments. Beginning with the days of Enosh,*[2] *when idol worship came into existence, opinions in the matter of faith fell into confusion. Some people denied the essentials of faith by saying that the world is eternal; "they denied Hashem, and said: It is not He" [Who called the world into existence] (see Yirmiyah 5:12). Others denied His knowledge of specific matters [in this world], "And they say, How can God know? Is there knowledge in the Most High? (Tehillim 73:11). Still others conceded His knowledge but denied the principle of providence — [that He is involved in this world] — and they made "men like the [helpless] fish of the sea" (Chavakkuk 1:14), [believing] that God does not watch over them and that there is no punishment or reward for their deeds. They say, "Hashem has forsaken the land" (Yechezkel 8:12).*
>
> *Now whenever God regards a group or an individual favorably and He does a miracle with them — by bringing about a change in the customary and natural order of the world — then the emptiness of all these [beliefs] becomes clear to all. A wondrous miracle demonstrates that the world has a God, that [this God] created it, that He knows [its affairs],*

2. See *Bereishis* (4:26): "To Shes was... born a son, and he named him Enosh. It was then that [God's Name] was profaned (*huchal*), by [people] calling [men and idols] by the Name of Hashem." Rashi there comments: "'It was then' — The word *huchal* is a term related to *chullin*, which means 'profane matters.' That is, [people began] calling the names of men and the names of idols after the Name of the Holy One, making them the objects of idolatrous worship and calling them deities." This is supported by one reading of the *Targum* which renders the verse thus: "In his days it became trite to pray using God's Name"; meaning, people ceased praying to God. See also above, Chapter Three, "In the days of Enosh...."

that He supervises it, and that He has the power to change it. And if, in addition, that wonder was foretold by a prophet then yet another principle is established — the truth of prophecy: "That God does speak with man" (Devarim 5:21) and that "He reveals His secret to His servants the prophets" (Amos 3:7), and thereby the whole Torah is confirmed.[3] *This is why [the Torah] says in connection with the wonders [in Egypt]: "So that you [Pharaoh] will realize that I am Hashem right here on earth" (Shemos 8:18).*

— Ramban, Shemos 13:16

When we read the full verse with which the Ramban closes, we can easily see how it demonstrates God's control of the world: "For if you do not release My people, I am going to incite a horde of wild beasts against you, your servants, your people and your houses. The houses of the Egyptians will be filled with wild beasts, as well as the ground on which they stand. On that day I will set apart the land of Goshen where My people are situated, that there not be any wild beasts there, so that you will realize that I am Hashem right here on earth" (*Shemos* 8:17-18).

All this teaches us the principle of providence; that is, that God has not abandoned the world to chance, as [the heretics] would have it.

D. Another example of God's supervision

Concerning the plague of wild beasts, Ramban writes:

"On that day I will set apart the land of Goshen" (Shemos 8:18): Since the first few plagues were not migratory in nature, it was no wonder that they occurred only in the land of Egypt and did not occur in the land of Goshen [where the Jews lived]. But this [plague of wild beasts] was

3. As was the case in Egypt. God gave prophecy to Moshe and Aharon and informed them of every upcoming plague. They then warned Pharaoh about each plague in advance, yet he was incapable of preventing it. Clearly, God had really spoken to them.

a migratory plague [because it consisted of animals that move about]. Thus when the wild beasts came up "from the lions' dens and from the mountains of the leopards" (see Shir HaShirim 4:8), and brought ruin upon the whole land of Egypt, [we would have expected them to] follow their nature and enter the land of Goshen as well.... Therefore it was necessary for [God] to say, "on that day I will set apart the land of Goshen" — so that it would be completely protected [from the wild beasts] — because "My people are situated" there, as most of [the people who lived there] were the Israelites.

"I will perform an act of redemption (p'dus) [to differentiate] between My people and your people" (Shemos 8:19): The intent of this verse is that even in the land of Egypt, if the beasts happen to find an individual Jew, they will not harm him. Instead, they will devour [only] the Egyptians, as it is written, "He sent against them a mixture of beasts that devoured them" (Tehillim 78:45), for this is what the word "p'dus," to differentiate, connotes. [Thus this verse] is similar [in content] to the verse, "I gave Egypt as your ransom, and Cush and Seba in your place" (Yeshayah 43:3).

— Ramban, Commentary to Shemos 13:16

Wild animals seldom enter inhabited areas, and when they do, they must be hungry and looking for food. Now, different species of animals subsist on different types of food; furthermore, animals of one species fear those that belong to a stronger species, for they instinctively know that they may be mauled by the stronger ones — especially when they are hungry. In short, it is naturally impossible for animals of all the different species to band together. Who, then, gathered them all — against their nature — at one appointed hour? Who identified the Egyptians for them? And who told them which of the homes were Egyptian and which were Jewish? It was an outright miracle in which everyone clearly witnessed God's providence upon earth!

E. A sign that God created the world

Concerning the plague of hail it is written: "There was hail, with fire blazing within the hail; it was very heavy — the likes of which had never been in all the land of Egypt since it had become a nation" (*Shemos* 9:24). *Rashi,* from *Shemos Rabbah* (12), explains: "This was a miracle within a miracle, for fire and hail mingled although hail is water! Yet in order to fulfill the Creator's will, they made peace with each other." The first miracle was the fact that there was hail in Egypt. That on its own was a miracle, as the Ibn Ezra notes: "It is known that even today hail and rain never fall on Egypt.... This is why they were very frightened, because the only [precipitation they were used to] comes as dew." Or, as the Ramban puts it, "But in the land of Egypt where it never rains or hails, it was a great wonder" (*Ramban, Shemos* 9:18). All the more so since it was a very heavy hail "the likes of which had never been in all the land." The second miracle was the fact that there was "fire blazing within the hail." "This was a wonder within a wonder" (*Ibn Ezra, Shemos* 9:24).

The hail devastated Egypt yet did not affect the Jews at all, as we see in these verses: "Throughout the land of Egypt the hail struck down everything that was in the field — both people and animals. The hail also struck down all the plants of the field and smashed all the trees of field. Only in the land of Goshen, where the Children of Israel were, was there no hail" (*Shemos* 9:25-26). This distinction was also a wonder:

> *"Only in the land of Goshen, where the Children of Israel were, was there no hail" (Shemos 9:26) — Because Moshe had stretched forth his hand toward heaven and brought down the hail, it should have followed that it would also come down upon the land of Goshen, as its air and Egypt's air are the same. Therefore [the Torah] explained that the air over the land of Goshen was saved [from the hail] because the Children of Israel were there.*
>
> *— Ramban, Shemos 9:26*

Thus God showed complete mastery over nature, and He thereby also showed that the world was created new — as the Ramban writes:

> *"... so that you will realize that the world belongs to Hashem" (Shemos 9:29) — this verse informs us of the principle of creation, for the reason everything is His is because He created everything out of nothing.*
>
> *— Ramban, Shemos 13:16*

F. The principle of God's absolute power

Another principle that Pharaoh was to learn from the plagues, and which is still a lesson for us, is the principle that God has absolute power over the world:

> *"So that you will realize that there is none like Me in the whole world" (Shemos 9:14). This indicates His might, i.e., that He rules over everything and that there is nothing that can restrain Him. The Egyptians either denied or doubted all of these principles, [while the miracles confirmed their truth].*
>
> *Accordingly, the great signs and wonders performed [in Egypt] constitute "faithful witnesses" (Yeshayah 8:2) to the truth of the existence of the Creator and to the truths of the whole Torah.*
>
> *— Ramban, Shemos 13:16*

The Ibn Ezra quotes Rabbi Yehudah HaLevi who describes all the plagues of Egypt in terms of God's absolute control over everything that exists:

> *There were two plagues in the water; the first was that the water turned red (causing the fish to die[4]), and the sec-*

4. The Seforno points out that "the water did not just appear like blood, but rather it looked and had the composition of actual blood, which is why 'the fish died.'" The fact that the water turned red was not enough to demonstrate that the water had really changed, but since the fish died, it demonstrated that the water had chemically changed into real blood; sleight of hand can fool the people but it can't fool the fish into dying!

ond was that the frogs came up from it. On the land there were two plagues; the first was the lice, and the second was the horde of wild beasts, which come from the earth as is written, "The earth shall produce living creatures" (Bereishis 1:24). Two came from the air; [the first is] pestilence, for it is caused by unusually hot or cold [air] and... because life depends on air, and the second was the plague of boils [which came when Moshe threw handfuls of furnace soot heavenward (see Shemos 9:8)] and the [Torah] calls the air over their heads "heaven." The seventh plague [hail] came from a combination of the sphere of storm and the sphere of fire, as is written, "fire blazing within the hail" (ibid. v. 24). The eighth plague, locusts, was [a plague] that came from afar through the wind. The ninth [darkness] was a wondrous plague in which the light from the two luminaries and from the stars did not [shine] on the land of Egypt. And the tenth was when the destructive force descended from the sphere of Glory to kill the firstborn.

— Ibn Ezra, Commentary to Shemos 9:1

Thus, the plagues encompassed all the realms of creation: water, land, air; earth, water, wind, and fire; inanimate objects, vegetation, living creatures, and humans. In short, it affected all of heaven and earth in order to show the Creator's exclusive control over everything.

G. Why are "testimonial mitzvos" so important?

Now that we have seen how many lessons of Torah faith were conveyed by the miracles associated with the Exodus, we can appreciate the Ramban's final remarks in his discussion of the significance of *tefillin*:

And because the Holy One, Blessed is He, does not make signs and wonders in every generation for the eyes of every wicked man or heretic [to teach all these lessons],

He therefore commanded us that we should always make a memorial or sign [through such physical mitzvos as tefillin, the Pesach offering, etc.] of that which we have seen with our eyes, and that we should transmit the matter to our children, and their children, and their children to their children, to the generations to come. He was very strict in this matter [because of the important lessons of faith that are carried by these mitzvos], as is indicated by the fact that one is liable to [spiritual] extinction (kareis) for eating leavened bread on Pesach, and for neglecting the Pesach offering. He has further required of us that we inscribe upon our arms and between our eyes all the signs and wonders that we have seen, and to inscribe them upon the doorposts of our houses as well. And we are to remember the [Exodus] by recital in the morning and evening — as the Rabbis have said (Berachos 21a): "The recital of 'True and firm' [which follows the Shema in the morning], is a Torah obligation because it is written, 'in order that you remember the day you left the land of Egypt all the days of your life'" (Devarim 16:3). [He further required] that we make a succah (booth) every year and many other commandments which are all memorials to the Exodus from Egypt. All these commandments are designed for the purpose that in all generations we should have testimonies to the wonders [that God performed] so that they should not be forgotten and so that no heretic will be able to open his lips to deny the belief in [the existence of] God.

— Ramban, Shemos 13:16

The Ramban concludes:

Through the great open miracles, one comes to acknowledge the hidden miracles which constitute the foundation of the whole Torah, for no one can have a part in the Torah of our teacher Moshe unless he believes that all our circumstances and incidents are miraculous; there is noth-

ing "natural" or "ordinary" about them — whether they are events that affect the public or the individual.

Instead, if a person observes the commandments, His reward will bring him success, and if he violates them, his punishment will cause his extinction. Everything is by decree of the Most High.

— Ramban, Shemos 13:16

H. The Exodus demonstrated the extent of God's knowledge of human affairs

The Exodus from Egypt, then, is fundamental to our faith and to the Torah. It showed the world that God rules over everything, thereby refuting the notion held by many heretics that God abandoned the earth and handed it over to the government of "officers." It refuted the notion held by the philosophers who thought that God's glory cannot possibly dwell on earth, for God — they thought — is too lofty to be concerned with lowly matters. But the Exodus showed that the Holy One does supervise the world and that He has thorough knowledge of all that transpires in this world. In particular, the plague of the firstborn demonstrated that God sees even the most lowly matters because in order to strike at the firstborn, He had to know which of the Egyptians were really firstborn and where they lived or where they were hiding: "If there was a firstborn [in the house], he died: if there was no firstborn there, then the chief person in the house died because the chief person in the house is called a *bechor* ('the first one').... Another opinion is that the Egyptian women were unfaithful to their husbands and bore children from young, unmarried men; thus there were many firstborn sons [in Egypt] — sometimes one woman could have as many as five 'firstborn' sons, each being the firstborn to his [true] father" (*Rashi* to *Shemos* 12:30). Thus it was shown to all that God's providence and supervision extend to people's most hidden and secret behavior: "I am the One Who distinguished in Egypt between one who was a firstborn and one who was not" (*Rashi* to *Bamidbar* 15:41).

I. Evidence of the Exodus

To this day, we can still see a trace of the wonders of the Exodus. For example, there is remaining evidence of the plague of locusts, as the Ramban writes in the name of Rabbeinu Chananel:

> *Ever since our teacher Moshe prayed [for the removal of the locusts], locusts have not caused devastating damage to the entire land of Egypt. Even when they invade the Land of Israel and proceed toward the Egyptian border, they do not completely devour the produce of [Egypt]. This is a well-known [phenomenon]. Now, in the case of the frogs, where Moshe said, "They will remain only in the river" (Shemos 8:5), [they] have indeed remained in the river till now; yet in the case of the locusts it is written, "There remained not one locust in all the border of Egypt" (ibid. 10:19). It is of a phenomenon of this kind that Scripture says, "Speak of all His wonders" (Tehillim 105:2).*
>
> — *Ramban, Commentary to Shemos 10:14*

In the preceding paragraphs we have only mentioned a few of the miracles associated with the Exodus, but there were many, many more that are described in the Haggadah and in the Midrashim. Rabbi Akiva expounded: "In Egypt they were afflicted with fifty plagues and on the Sea they were afflicted with two hundred fifty plagues!" (*Mechilta, Beshalach* §6). Together, they teach the fundamentals of Torah faith which is why it is so important that we not forget them.

J. The message of these mitzvos is beyond doubt

We are therefore commanded to keep certain action-based mitzvos, in order to instill within ourselves an everlasting awareness of God's supervision. We have no doubts about what these mitzvos symbolize because we have kept them throughout the generations. We don the same *tefillin* that God showed Moshe, and that Moshe showed the rest of Israel, and so on from generation to generation. Likewise, we keep the mitzvos of Shabbos and the Yamim Tovim just as our ancestors did. And though the Jews have been repeatedly scattered in exile to all ends of the world, yet when Jews of one exile meet up with Jews who arrived from another exile, they see that they have all been keeping the same mitzvos. Furthermore, the Jews have always been a wise and discerning people — "the People of the Book" — and Jews are such critics! How, then, is it conceivable that Jews would keep these mitzvos unless they were sure of their authenticity and unless they were sure that the entire Exodus narrative has been accurately transmitted from father to son throughout the generations? Every year since the Exodus Jews have fulfilled the mitzvos of Pesach and of the Seder night; they recline at the table, and they recount the story of the Exodus to their children. Jews have been burned at the stake and their blood has been spilled, yet the Jews continue to ascend and sanctify the Name of Heaven, always recounting His wondrous deeds. We are not willing to exchange Him for the vanity of the nations.

K. We recount the story frequently and intensely

Another reason why we do not doubt the story of the Exodus is because of the frequency and intensity with which we recount its events. On the Seder night there is a mitzvah to recount the story of the Exodus — especially to one's children — as we learn from the verse, "Tell it to your son" (*Shemos* 13:8). The mitzvah is to recount as many details of the Exodus as possible and to act as though one is actually leaving Egypt at that very moment. Thus our Sages taught, "The more one elaborates upon the story of the departure from Egypt, the more he is praised" (*Pesach Haggadah*). In addition, there is a separate obligation to remember the Exodus every day of the year, as is written (*Shemos* 13:3), "Remember this day that you went out of Egypt, out of the house of slavery, for with a mighty hand Hashem took you out of here," upon which Rashi comments: "This teaches that we mention the Exodus from Egypt every day."

The Gemara (*Berachos* 12b) teaches: "We mention the Exodus of Egypt at night [as well]... as is written (*Devarim* 16:3), 'In order that you remember the day you left the land of Egypt all the days of your life': 'the days of your life' — these are the days; 'all the days of your life' — these are the nights." This is the halachah, as the Rambam writes (*Hilchos Krias Shema* 1:3): "And it is a mitzvah to mention the Exodus from Egypt both by day and by night, as is written, 'In order that you remember the day you left the land of Egypt all the days of your life.'" Furthermore, the Gemara (*Berachos* 21a) rules: "If one has a doubt whether or not he recited 'True and certain' [the third and final blessing of the *Shema*]... he must recite it again.... Why? because 'True and certain' is a Torah obligation."[5] Rashi there explains that the blessing of 'True and certain' is a Torah obligation "because it mentions the Exodus from Egypt, which is a Torah obligation as is written, 'In order that you remember the day you left the land of Egypt.'"

L. More miracles on the way out

The miracles of the Exodus did not end with our release from Egyptian bondage; the very way in which we departed was miraculous, as we read in the book of *Shemos* (12:37): "The Children of Israel traveled from Rameses to Succos." Rashi, from the *Mechilta*, explains: "'From Rameses to Succos' — These were distant from one another 120 mil and yet they reached there in one moment ['in the blink of an eye,' *Mechilta*], as it is said (ibid. 19:4), 'And I carried you on wings of eagles.'" On this latter verse Rashi comments: "'And I carried you' — This happened on that day when the Israelites came to Rameses because the Israelites were living dispersed throughout the whole district of Goshen and in one brief moment — when they had gathered to travel and leave

5. See also *Tosafos* there who maintains that the same rule applies when someone has a doubt concerning the paragraph of *tzitzis,* because "anything that [discusses] the Exodus from Egypt is called 'True and certain.'"

— they all gathered together at Rameses."[6] This miracle, as well, has a corresponding mitzvah: in *Devarim* (16:3) it says, "You must not eat anything leavened with it, and on its account you shall eat matzos, the bread of affliction, for a seven-day period, for you left the land of Egypt in haste. [This is] in order that you remember the day you left the land of Egypt all the days of your life." From the plain reading of the verse it appears that the obligation to remember the Exodus includes not only the fact that we left Egypt but also the way we left, for by doing so we emphasize the fact that the Exodus was completely miraculous. Another indication of the significance of this last miracle is the fact that of all the miracles which God performed for the Jews, He highlighted this one in the introduction He gave before giving us the Torah: "I carried you on wings of eagles." By nature, a journey of this magnitude, involving an entire nation on a long trek, should have required a very long time, yet it was done "in the blink of an eye." God gathered them like a shepherd who gathers his young lambs, and He lifted them like a compassionate eagle does for his offspring, placing them onto His Clouds of Glory. And then, like a father who joyfully brings his children home, He took them "home" — to Mount Sinai. "I carried you on wings of eagles and brought you to Me" (*Shemos* 19:4).

---

6. Although these two comments of Rashi seem to contradict each other — one says that they gathered from all over Goshen to Rameses while the other say that they traveled 120 mil from Rameses to Succos — the *Sifsei Chachamim* explains that both are true; first they gathered to Rameses and then they traveled to Succos, all in a moment or two.

CHAPTER SEVEN

Krias Yam Suf

The Splitting of the Sea of Reeds

A. The Miracles at the Sea were greater than the miracles in Egypt

Many people view *Krias Yam Suf*, the Splitting of the Sea of Reeds, as part of the events and miracles of *Yetzias Mitzraim*, the Exodus from Egypt. But the Torah and our Sages considered it as a separate set of miracles performed by God for the Jewish people.[1] Moreover, the mira-

1. In the Torah, this can be seen from a careful reading of *Shemos* 12:41 and 13:17-18. This distinction is even clearer in the works of our Sages, as can be seen from the sources discussed in this chapter.

cles at the Sea surpassed the miracles of the Exodus. Our Sages in the Haggadah (and in the *Mechilta, Beshalach* §6) point out that there were five times as many miracles at the Sea as there were in Egypt. They derived this by comparing two verses: "Of the plagues in Egypt, it says: (*Shemos* 8:15), 'The sorcerers said to Pharaoh, "It is a finger of God!"' while at the Sea, it is said, 'And Israel saw the great hand which Hashem had used upon Egypt.'" In Egypt the miracles were only like a "finger" but at the Sea they were like a "hand" of five "fingers." Using the same calculation, but starting with five afflictions per plague, Rabbi Akiva says in the Haggadah: "In Egypt the Egyptians were smitten with fifty plagues, while at the Sea they were smitten with two-hundred-and-fifty plagues." Another indication that the miracles at the Sea were of an entirely different order is the fact that the Jews did not sing when they departed Egypt but they did sing after experiencing the Splitting of the Sea. What had aroused them so? At the Sea they beheld fantastic wonders and visions of God's glory — "At the Sea, even the maidservants beheld things that [the prophet] Yechezkel did not get to see" (*Mechilta, Beshalach* §3), and the Divine Presence rested upon them, inspiring them to sing to God.

B. Ten major miracles

In *Avos* (5:4) we are taught that ten miracles occurred at the Sea, but the Mishnah does not elaborate. The Rambam, however, in his commentary to that Mishnah describes them in detail. The following is a summary of the Rambam's list of miracles: (1) the waters split; (2) the path went through the water, forming a tunnel straight through the sea; (3) the sea floor became hard so that they could walk on it, and it did not remain muddy; (4) when the Egyptians walked on the floor, it was very muddy and it stuck to their feet; (5) the sea split into several parallel paths (tunnels) for each of the tribes; (6) the water became as hard as stones, so that the heads of the Egyptians would shatter against them; (7) the water did not harden into one solid unit but into many pieces, giving the appearance of a wall built of neatly arranged bricks; (8) when the water solidified, it was absolutely clear and the people of one tribe could see the members of the other tribes (who were walking in their own tunnels) through the water as though they were looking through crystal-clear glass; (9) sweet water flowed out of the walls so the Jews would have what to drink; and (10) the above mentioned drinking water froze as soon as it was not needed, so that nobody would be harmed by it.

Some of the other miracles at the Sea were the punishments meted out there to the Egyptians. After a careful reading of *Shemos* (15:5), Rashi concludes that the Egyptians afflicted at the Sea suffered to different degrees, depending on the level of wickedness with which they enslaved the Jews: The most wicked became like "straw" — they were violently tossed about in the water to prolong their suffering; the intermediate became like "stone" — they sank but not very quickly; and the least evil among them became like "lead" — they died quickly.

C. The miracle of dry land

As we mentioned above, one of the major miracles of the Splitting of the Sea was the fact that the seabed became hard and dry — "The Children of Israel had walked on dry land in the middle of the sea" (*Shemos* 14:29). This miracle was actually a double miracle, as the Ibn Ezra explains:

> *The reason [the Torah] repeats this verse, [once in verse 22 and again here in verse 29], is because Pharaoh was drowning while there were still Jews passing through the Sea. This was a wonder within a wonder, for wherever the Israelites were walking there was an easterly wind drying out the water, but wherever Pharaoh and his army went there was a different wind melting the water that had previously hardened into walls. Thus, there were simultaneously two kinds of wind in the Sea in close proximity. [Verse 29, then, should be understood as a continuation of verse 28: "The water fell back again and covered over the chari-*

ots and cavalrymen of Pharaoh's entire army... while at the same time the Children of Israel walked on dry land."]
— *Ibn Ezra, Commentary to Shemos 14:29*

The miracle of the dry land was significant not only because it was a great wonder but also because it caused the complete downfall of the Egyptians. The Ramban elaborates:

"Moshe then raised his hand over the Sea, and Hashem drove the Sea with a powerful east wind the whole night [and turned the Sea to dry land]" (Shemos 14:21). It was His will, may He be blessed, to divide the Sea by a strong wind, making it appear as if the wind dried the Sea. [Winds from the east are very dry] as seen from the verse, "An east wind shall come, the wind of Hashem coming up from the wilderness, and his spring shall become dry, and his fountains shall be dried up" (Hoshea 13:15). In this manner He caused the Egyptians to err and cause their own destruction, for because of this [wind] they thought that perhaps it was the wind which made the Sea into dry land, and not God's power that did this for the sake of Israel. And although wind never splits a sea into sections, their desire to harm them was so great that they paid no attention to this, and they followed the Israelites into the Sea. This is the intent of the expressions: "And I will strengthen Pharaoh's resolve.... And they will enter [the Sea] after them" (Shemos 14:4 and 17). He hardened their hearts [so that each one] would say: "I will pursue my foes and I will overtake them" (Tehillim 18:38).... They forgot that "it is Hashem Who is fighting for them against the Egyptians" (Shemos 14:25).
— *Ramban, Commentary to Shemos 14:21*

D. The Egyptians were punished with their own plot

The general principle that emerged at the Sea was that Divine providence operates by giving each person what he deserves, based on his actions, for the Children of Israel received salvation and love while the wicked Egyptians received retribution "by the very thing that they plotted against [Israel]" (*Shemos* 18:11). The Egyptian's plot was to cast the Israelite babies into the water, but now they were the ones sentenced to drown: "They were cooked in the same pot in which they had cooked others" (*Shemos Rabbah* 1:9).

In order to punish each Egyptian with what he deserved, God infused the water with intelligence so that it could "know" how to treat each one. The Torah alludes to this in the verse (*Shemos* 15:8), "By the breath of Your nostrils the waters were piled up (ne'ermu)," which is rendered by Onkelos as: "By the word of Your mouth the waters became wise," because the word *ne'ermu* is related to the word *armah*, which means cunning. This can be better understood with the commentary of the Gaon of Vilna:

> *"By the breath of Your nostrils the waters were piled up (ne'ermu)" – Man was hewn of physical matter, but the Holy One was kind to him and "blew into his nostrils the soul of life; thus man became an [intelligent] living being" (Bereishis 2:7), and Man thereby gained wisdom and intelligence. Here, too, the waters of Yam Suf gained intelligence, which is why it says: "By the breath of Your nostrils" that You blew into the water, "the water became wise" (ne'ermu) — as Onkelos renders: "The waters became wise."*
>
> *— Kol Eliyahu, Beshalach [paragraph 61]*

What was the "intelligence" of the water? That it "knew" which punishment each of the Egyptians deserved!

Yisro, who at one time was the idolatrous "priest of Midyan" – and had tried every form of pagan worship in the world — was aroused to convert mainly because of the Splitting of the Sea. When Yisro came to the Jews in the desert, he exclaimed: "Now I know that Hashem is greater than the gods [worshiped by all] others, for they were [punished] by the very thing that [the Egyptians] had plotted against [Israel]" (*Shemos* 18:11). Rashi there explains: "The [Egyptians] had plotted to destroy them by water and they were themselves destroyed by water."

With this principle, the Ramban explains why the Egyptians deserved such a harsh punishment:

> *The verse means to say that because "[the Egyptians were punished] by the very thing that they had plotted against [Israel]," it is now obvious to me "that Hashem is greater than all gods." The elucidation of this is as follows: Considering the fact that God had decreed upon Israel, "[The inhabitants] will enslave them and oppress them" (Bereishis 15:13), no great punishment should have been meted out to the Egyptians. However, the [Egyptians] were excessively wicked toward [Israel] and had planned to eradicate them from the world, as they said, "Come, let us deal cleverly with them, so that they do not increase" (Shemos 1:10). Pharaoh decreed upon the midwives to kill the male children, and he commanded his people, "Every boy that is born you shall cast into the River" (ibid. v. 22). This is why the Egyptians deserved the harsh punishment of annihilation. It is this principle which is expressed in His words, "And I will also carry out judgment on the nation that will enslave them" (Bereishis 15:14), as I explained earlier. God, though, saw their plot and took vengeance upon them for the wickedness in their hearts. Scripture [elsewhere] reiterates, "You imposed signs and wonders upon Pharaoh... for You knew that they had sinned willfully against them" (Nechemia 9:10).*

For Yisro, this event was ample evidence that there is Divine providence and that God is unique in the way He judges.

E. "Measure for measure" — the fundamental principle of Divine retribution

The verse from Nechemia, quoted above by the Ramban, continues with the effect this judgment had on the world: "And You brought for Yourself renown, as clear as this very day" (*Nechemia* 9:10). The Splitting of the Sea made everyone realize how great

God is because it demonstrated that when God punishes man He does so "measure for measure." This was a significant revelation for people, for it is the most fundamental principle of Divine retribution, as we will now discuss.

We have learned in the Mishnah (*Avos* 2:6): "[Hillel once] saw a skull floating on the water; he said to it: 'Because you drowned others, they drowned you; and those who drowned you will be drowned eventually.'" The Rambam there explains:

> *The meaning of this passage is that evil actions tend to return upon the head of those who do them, as Scripture says (Mishlei 5:22), "The iniquities of the wicked one will trap him...." And as another verse says (Tehillim 7:16), "He has dug a pit, and dug it deep, only to fall into his own trap." Our Sages put it this way (Sotah 8b), "In the same measuring [utensil] used by a person to measure — he himself is measured." This fact can be verified in all eras and places: whenever a wicked person develops a new form of iniquity or contemptible behavior, he himself ends up being harmed by the very evil he developed. In effect, a wicked person punishes himself, for he teaches others new methods of evil, which they can then use to harm him and others. Conversely, anyone who teaches positive behavior, and develops new ways of doing good, will ultimately benefit from his own innovation, for once people know to do that good, they will do it to him and to others. The words of the verse, then, are perfect (Iyov 34:11): "The deeds of a man repay him."*
>
> *— Rambam, Commentary to Avos 2:6*

But when nature itself is used to punish a person, it shows clearly that his punishment was not merely the simple consequence of harming others. When a wicked person is punished by the natural world in precisely the same manner that he sinned, it shows that the events of this world are not arbitrary. Thus when people are punished "measure for measure," it shows that there is "an eye that sees" (*Avos* 2:1) and that there is a Judge Who makes each person pay for his deeds. When a person realizes this, he comes to greater levels of faith in God. This is how Yisro realized that "Hashem is greater than the gods [worshiped by all] others" (*Shemos* 18:11) — for God used His absolute control over the water, land and air to punish the Egyptians exactly in accord with their deeds. Yisro knew that only the true God could do such a thing, as the Seforno explains:

> *With this [Divine retribution, God] showed His superiority over all the elohim (the angels and angel-officers) because no nation ever thought that their god could use everything [in the world] to pay "measure for measure"; all they ever claimed was that their [god] could do the one specific action unique to it.*
>
> — *Seforno, Commentary to Shemos 18:11*

Yisro, who had worshiped every type of idol worship, and knew all their claims, now saw that God's hand controls everything. In this manner God brought for himself "renown, as clear as this very day" (*Nechemia* 9:10).

F. The Splitting of the Sea was most certainly not a natural event

Some heretics maintain a theory that they believe "rationally" explains the Splitting of the Sea. Now, although it is a completely illogical and unscientific theory, it is still our duty to refute it because King Shlomo taught (*Mishlei* 26:5): "Answer a fool according to his foolishness," which, as our Sages explain (see *Shabbos* 30b), is an instruction to respond to arguments when the issue is Torah lessons. We will therefore devote a few words to this matter.

According to the heretics' theory, what transpired at the Sea of Reeds was simply a natural phenomenon caused by a sudden shift from high tide to low tide. Moshe, they further theorize, somehow knew that this was about to occur and wisely took advantage of this natural phenomenon to cross during the low point.

Like many theories put forth by heretics, there is no evidence for this theory whatsoever; it is pure conjecture. As such, we wonder how a heretic would respond to the following points:

(1) How do you know that this event ever took place? The only way you know about it is from the Torah's account of it and from what is known of it in world history — and you cannot ignore what is well known. How, then, can you claim that the event happened differently than the way it appears in the tradition itself?

(2) The phenomenon of high and low tides is merely the natural cycle of the rising and falling of the sea. At most it can cause a tidal wave (such as the kind mentioned in the Gemara — see *Bava Metzia* 21b), but has anyone ever heard of a sea vanishing, falling so low that an entire nation of millions of people — men women and children, with all their possessions — would be able to cross it? Furthermore, if the Splitting of the Sea was a natural phenomenon, as they claim, then it should have recurred at some other point during the course of history, since all of nature repeats itself — "He established [the laws of nature] forever and ever, He issued a decree that will not change" (*Tehillim* 148:6). Why, then, has this not occurred at any other time — not before and not since, not in this sea nor in any other sea?

(3) If this was a one-time, but natural, event the Jews should have been very afraid to cross the sea, for they had no experience with such a phenomenon and had no way of knowing when the water would suddenly swell up again. Furthermore, transporting an entire nation is not a quick process, so how could Moshe be so sure that this unparalleled quirk of nature would last long enough?

(4) Seabeds are not perfectly flat; they are full of muddy peaks and valleys and all sorts of obstacles. How, then, were the Jews able to walk across it?

(5) How do they explain all the other miracles associated with the Splitting of the Sea?

We who possess true faith are not troubled by these questions; instead, the Splitting of the Sea only intensifies our faith in God and His might.

CHAPTER EIGHT

The Hidden Miracles of Special Providence

A. "Hidden" vs. "open" miracles

Earlier (in Chapter Six, The Exodus From Egypt) we learned from the Ramban that open miracles force people to acknowledge the hidden miracles of life:

Through the great open miracles, one comes to acknowledge the hidden miracles which constitute the foundation of the whole Torah, for no one can have a part in the Torah of our teacher Moshe unless he believes that all our circumstances and incidents are miraculous; there is nothing "natural" or "ordinary" about them — whether they are events that affect the public or the individual. Instead, if a person observes the commandments, His reward will bring him success, but if he violates them, His punishment will cause his extinction. Everything is by decree of the Most High.

— Ramban, Shemos 13:16

But what are hidden miracles, and when do they occur? These are the questions we will address in this chapter.

B. Miracles that masquerade as nature

When people refer to an event as "a miracle" — such as the miracle of the Exodus — they mean to say that the event was so out of the ordinary that it was clearly an act of God. That type of miracle is what we call an open miracle because it is not shrouded in nature. Conversely, a hidden miracle is an act of God that is "dressed up" in nature; that is, it gives the appearance of being an ordinary event. But since the miracle is only masquerading behind nature, it is possible to look at it carefully and see through the costume. For the person who does this, the "hidden" miracle suddenly becomes an "exposed" miracle, for he sees that there is nothing "normal" or "ordinary" about the event. This is especially true of the person who benefited directly from the miracle. He is much more likely to realize that his experience was a miracle, for he knows better than others that the action he took could never have naturally brought about such wondrous results. With a little contemplation, we can see that, in fact, all of nature is really a (hidden) miracle, as the Ramban points out:

Reward and punishment in this world, as mentioned throughout the Torah, are all miracles, but they are hidden. They appear to the onlooker as being part of the natural order of things, but in truth, they come upon man as punishment and reward [for deeds]. It is for this reason that

the Torah speaks at great length of the assurances concerning this world... These are wonders that go contrary to nature.
— *Ramban, Commentary to Shemos 6:2*

C. Hidden miracles in the lives of our forefathers

The Torah is replete with allusions to this sort of miracle. The Torah's assurances and admonitions and most of its stories — from the lives of the forefathers to the concluding stories of the Jews in the Desert — are all examples of "hidden" miracles. Let us examine a few of these episodes.

Twice, a king took Sarah Imeinu from Avraham (the first time it was done by Pharaoh and the second time by Avimelech), and in both cases, the king that took her was prevented from doing any harm. When Pharaoh tried harming her, "Hashem then brought tremendous plagues on Pharaoh and his household" (*Bereishis* 12:17); and when Avimelech took her, he was told in a dream, "You are going to die on account of the woman you have taken, for she is someone's wife" (ibid. 20:3). Thus "[Hashem] allowed no man to rob them, and he rebuked kings for their sake: 'Dare not touch My anointed ones, and to My prophets do no harm'" (*I Divrei HaYamim* 16:21-22). In the end, both kings were forced to send off Avraham and Sarah with wealth and honor, and Avimelech and his general Pichol were forced to concede to Avraham, "God is with you in everything you do" (*Bereishis* 21:22). Rashi explains: "[They said this] because they saw that he had left the locality of Sodom safely, that he had fought against the kings and that they had fallen into his hands, and that his wife had been remembered in his old age."

All of these events that occurred for Avraham's sake were garbed in either natural events or human actions. However, with a little contemplation, it was possible to see that it was God's providence that guided and brought about those wonders. Avraham witnesses the overturning of Sodom and sees that the only ones who are saved are his relatives, Lot and his daughters; he wages a war against four mighty kings with their armies — and wins —

despite their overwhelming power; many people have children, but Avraham and Sarah have a child in their old age when it should have been impossible for them to have children anymore. Having relatives who escape calamity, winning a war, and having children are all events that happen without miracles, yet those who were interested in the truth saw that "God is with you in everything you do."

Indeed, God was "with" Avraham not only by extending Divine assistance to him, but also by overriding nature for him:

> *"[Hashem] took him outside" (Bereishis 15:5). Its Midrashic explanation is: Go out of your astrological [fate] — that which you saw in your constellation that you will not raise a son; Avram has no son but Avraham will have a son… I will give you a new name, and your mazal-destiny will be changed.*
>
> — *Rashi, Commentary to Bereishis 15:5*

D. Hidden miracles for the Jewish people

The Jews in the Desert were promised that their entry into the Land of Israel would be accompanied by blessings:

> *You shall serve Hashem, your God, and He will bless your bread and your water; and I will eliminate [any] illness from among you. There will be no woman who miscarries or is childless in your land. I will grant you your full number of years. I will let the fear of Me go before you, and the entire nation among whom you come, I will throw into confusion; and I will make all your enemies turn [in retreat]. I will send tzir'ah-insects before you, and they will drive out the Chivvi, the Cana'ani and the Chitti from before you.*
>
> — *Shemos 23:25-28*

But this blessing was guaranteed only if they would eradicate idolatry from the land:

> *For My angel will go before you, and he will bring you to the Emori, the Chitti, the Perizzi, the Cana'ani, the Chivvi*

and the Yevusi, and I will annihilate them. You must not prostrate yourselves to their gods nor serve them, and you must not perform their practices; but you must eradicate [their gods] and demolish their idol-statues.
— Shemos 23:23-24

The words of the Ramban are illuminating:

"You shall serve Hashem, your God, and He will bless your food and your drink" (Shemos 23:25). The intention of this verse is as follows. Most idolaters acknowledge and know that the revered God is "the God of [all] powers and the Lord [over all] lords" (Devarim 10:17), and they do not intend to worship the idols themselves, but they think that these acts of worship will bring them success in their endeavors. Thus when they worship the sun it is because they found it to have beneficial power over their crops, and they find the moon to have influence over fountains and all deep waters, and similarly [they attribute powers] to all the hosts of the heaven. They are even more inclined to think that they will greatly benefit by worshipping the angels, since they are invested with dignity through ministering before the Great God.[1] *Therefore this verse states that only through the worship of the Holy One, Blessed is He, can you have success and protection, and the uprooting of idolatry will not cause damage: on the contrary, it will add goodness and blessing to you, for the Holy One will bless your "bread," this being a term which includes all manner of food, and will bless your "water," which is a generic term for all liquids that people drink. The blessing referred to [in the verse] means increase, so that you will have an abundance of them.*

"And I will eliminate [any] illness from among you." That is to say, through them [the bread and water that I will bless], I will free you from disease, for when your food and drink are good and healthy, they do not cause sick-

1. See above, Chapter Three.

nesses but, quite the contrary, heal you. And He states furthermore that "there will be no woman who miscarries" among you nor one who is childless "with shriveled breasts" (Hoshea 9:14), for when food and drink and the air are blessed, human bodies become healthy and the organs of reproduction are able to function properly....

"I will grant you your full number of years" (Shemos 23:26) means that one will not die prematurely in battle, nor through an epidemic caused by a change in the atmosphere, but only at a ripe age — whatever happens to be the normal span of life during that particular generation, such as seventy or eighty years as in the generation of King David (see Tehillim 90:10). I have already mentioned that these are all miracles, God showing "wonders in the heavens and in the earth" (Yoel 3:3) for the sake of those who do His will. And then He said that just as He will do on their behalf "a sign for good" (Tehillim 86:17), so will He do to their enemies for bad; He will give them "a frightened heart" (Devarim 28:65), "and in the recesses [of their hearts they will feel] dread" (ibid. 32:25). Moreover, He will send the tzir'ah amongst them, this being a kind of hornet of the family of the bee.... The meaning of this verse is that he will send it through the atmosphere of their land like the locust that he had sent in Egypt... "My great army" (Yoel 2:25), which came in the days of Yoel. The meaning of the expression, "I will send tzir'ah-insects before you, and they will drive out the Chivvi..." (Shemos 23:28), is that this will be the cause of their being driven out of the land, for since the hornets "will cover the face of the land" (ibid. 10:5) and darken it, they will not be able to go into battle.

— Ramban to Shemos 23:25-26

Here the Torah was discussing blessing and blight: God will bless the food, water, and air of the righteous and they will live long lives. At the same time, He will bring dread upon His enemies, which will prompt them to flee, and a natural disaster (the *tzir'ah* - insects) to hasten their downfall. These are all things that on the surface seem to be purely natural processes, yet they are miracles because they were only to happen through God's special alteration of the world and are based on merit or guilt. As the Ramban (quoted above) writes: "If a person observes the commandments, His reward will bring him success, but if he violates them, his punishment will cause his extinction."

Whether these hidden miracles are initially recognized as such or not, since "through the great open miracles, one comes to acknowledge the hidden miracles," the believer who acknowledges God's interaction with the world will sooner or later see how it was God's influence that brought about the blessing, courage and counsel for His "friends," and terror, dread, and confusion for His "foes."

E. Hidden miracles for individuals

What a person will do usually depends on the dictates of his heart and mind. But who tells the heart what to do? God does — "Like streams of water is the heart of a king in the hand of Hashem, wherever He wishes, so He directs it" (*Mishlei* 21:1). While every person has free will to choose a course of action, the outcome of those choices is determined by providence.[2]

Thus it is written (ibid. 19:21), "Many designs are in man's heart, but the counsel [*atzas*] of Hashem, only it will prevail." Designs are the numerous thoughts and plans that come to a person before taking action — at that point they are "many" — while counsel refers to the end result effected by the person's actions. Since the outcome always conforms to God's will — no matter what the person had originally planned — there can only be one "counsel" and "only it will prevail." For example, many people devise elaborate schemes for earning their living, but to be successful they have to choose the right one. Why are some people successful while others are not? What happens to all the schemes? The answer to these questions lies in the following verse (*Devarim*

---

2. See *Malbim,* Commentary to *Mishlei* 19:21 and to *Yeshayah* 14:24. -ed.

8:18): "You shall remember Hashem, your God, for it is He Who gives you the ability to amass wealth," or as Onkelos renders it, "for it is He Who gives you the counsel [*eitzah*] to amass wealth." Success or failure may seem to hinge completely on one's schemes, when in truth it depends on God's "counsel." Ultimately, each person receives only what he deserves as determined by God on Rosh Hashanah:

> *All the livelihood of a person is determined between Rosh Hashanah and Yom Kippur, except for the expenses of Shabbos, the expenses of Yamim Tovim, and the expenses of teaching his son Torah — in these, if a person subtracts, it is subtracted from him and if he adds, they give him more.*
> *— Beitzah 16a*

Whenever a person spends money for the sake of honoring God, he can expect God to "reimburse" him. The reimbursement may come through natural routes, but it is orchestrated by God to achieve His objective. For instance, God may plant favorable thoughts in the hearts of the shopkeeper, the merchant, or anyone else who is connected with this righteous person's livelihood. The result of this favorable treatment will be that he will receive exactly what was allotted to him. Conversely, if a person sins, he can lose the blessing that was previously allotted to him (on Rosh Hashanah) through an unexpected expense orchestrated by God.

F. Providence and the hidden miracles of war

Perhaps the easiest place to see God's providence is in war. The outcome of every war depends on the wisdom, strategy, and confidence of a nation's leadership and on the courage, determination, and morale of every soldier in the army. These are all matters that dwell in the domain of the heart — and in the hand of God. He alone determines what a nation's fate shall be — based on their merits or faults — and accordingly sets their hearts to conform to His plan.

The Jews were never guaranteed victory in their wars; instead, they experienced advances and setbacks, always in direct proportion to how they used their free will. A review of the wars recounted in Scripture consistently shows this correlation. They were completely victorious against the Egyptians, for at that time they were meritorious. But in their war against Amalek at Refidim, which occurred after they "tested and quarreled" against God (see *Shemos* 17), they were only partially successful in defeating Amalek. Later, after the sin of the Spies, they were warned, "Do not go up and do not battle" (*Devarim* 1:42) in Canaan. When they ignored this warning, they were smitten and "crushed as far as Chormah (destruction)" (*Bamidbar* 14:45). Of course, if they had not sinned at all they could have entered the land immediately and God would have granted them complete victory.

This pattern of merit-leads-to-victory and fault-leads-to-defeat continued throughout the period of the Judges and the Kings. Scripture consistently describes Israel's swing between victory and defeat as a direct consequence of either heeding or ignoring God's commands. For the Jews, then, what matters most in war is their spiritual standing.

G. Keeping the Torah stimulates special providence

Earlier, we studied the promises recorded in *Shemos* 23 using the commentary of the Ramban. From his comments, we learned that blessing only comes to a person when he follows God. From the comments of Rabbi Avraham Ibn Ezra we can gain some insight into how following God brings blessing:

> *[God] gives reward [for serving Him] in four ways: The first is "He will bless your bread and water"; the second is "I will eliminate [any] illness from among you"; the third is "There will be no woman who miscarries or is childless in your land"; and the fourth is "I will grant you your full number of years."*

The Ibn Ezra understood that the first two blessings, which relate to having a healthy body, are brought about by keeping the

Torah because when a person keeps the Torah it helps his soul control the body, making the body more healthy:

> *[God] gave the Torah in order to [help people] fortify their sublime soul against the rule of the body. However, if the Torah is not kept, then the body overcomes the soul. For example, from the study of physiology we know that if the red bile dominates a person's nature, he will have a temper.... Now, if the soul is not wise enough to withstand [the body] it will follow the body. The same can occur even to someone who does not normally have [internal] "heat" [and therefore does not normally have a temper], yet when someone insults or curses him it can generate heat (that he did not previously possess) until he becomes angry.*
>
> *But God, in His mercy, chose Israel and instructed them to keep the Torah. When they keep it, their wisdom is reinforced and it guides them along a straight path that takes them out of harm's way. Their bodies then obey the orders given by their soul — instead of the soul following the body. Then, when the soul is fortified, the force that preserves the body is also strengthened [as a gift] from Heaven.... Thus, a person who keeps the Torah has no need for a doctor together with God.*
>
> — *Ibn Ezra, Commentary to Shemos 23:25*

The third blessing, protection against miscarriage, can be seen more as an issue of mazal-fate than health. The Ibn Ezra therefore now addresses how "fate" plays no role in the life of someone who is attached to God:

> *I will now talk about the wisdom of astrology: Know that creatures that are born are subject to occurrences set by the [constellations] at the moment the person is born.... Now, the timing of when a woman was born will determine whether she will be included in the category of those who miscarry or those who are completely barren. However, if a person is attached to God, then — regardless of [her] time of birth*

and natural incapability of having children — the "Glorious Name" will strengthen the person's generative power ... and repair the person's sources of [fertility], enabling the person to bear children. Hashem therefore said to Avraham (Bereishis 17:1), "Walk before Me and be whole," or as our Sages said, "Go out of your astrological [fate]."

— Ibn Ezra, Commentary to Shemos 23:25

The fourth blessing, longevity, is dependent on inner health and on protection from external mishaps that cut life short. The Ibn Ezra now shows how keeping the Torah and being attached to God helps the person live without fear of death:

The fourth [blessing] is that the person will live many years. We know that each person has a set amount of time to live, and that this allotted life depends on the amount of natural "heat" and "moisture" [contained in the person].... But when a person is attached to the Name [of God], his soul sustains the body's heat and the moisture. In this manner, it is possible for a person to live longer than his allotted time. Thus it is written (Mishlei 11:27), "The fear of Hashem will increase days, but the years of the wicked will be shortened." And it is written (Yirmiyah 17:11), "In the middle of his days it will leave him." And it is written (I Shmuel 26:10), "Hashem will strike him with illness, or his day will come [and he will die]."

When a person dies at war or in a plague, we cannot say that the person died at his allotted time — as the consequence of "heat" and "moisture" — for these are circumstances that originate from the outside. Nevertheless, God, to Whom he was attached, will save him from them all.

— Ibn Ezra, Commentary to Shemos 23:26

This type of person is protected from all mishaps, for "The Name to Whom he is attached will bring about causes that will protect him from harm" (*Ibn Ezra* to *Shemos* 6:3). God will either give the person ideas that will help him escape or He will deflect the incidents away from him — such as in the verse (*Yeshayah* 43:3), "I gave Egypt as your ransom," and in (*Mishlei* 11:8), "The righteous one is removed from affliction, but the wicked one comes in his place."

H. Sidestepping mazal

Elsewhere, the Ibn Ezra gives another description of the difference between the system of nature — used for all the nations — and the system of specific providence — used for Israel. In this exposition, the Ibn Ezra explains how righteous people escape predetermined events:

> *All vegetation and living creatures on earth — the birds and animals, the beasts and the reptiles, and all people — are connected [to the higher creatures, such as the constellations and the angels].... The ministering [angels] cannot alter their course nor can they violate the set routine that God ordained for them. Then all the legions of heaven... conform to the same pattern. [Since their behavior is preset], they cannot act "good" or "bad."*
>
> *Furthermore, worshiping a heavenly body cannot help the worshiper, for whatever was decreed upon him — in accord with the way his constellation was arranged at the time of his birth — will happen to him. The only exception to this system is when a person is specially protected by the Supreme Power [i.e. God] against the power of the stars. To illustrate: Imagine that a constellation augured a flood (from an overflowing river) that would kill many people. Then a prophet came to the people and warned them to return to God before the calamity comes upon them, and they repented wholeheartedly. [Now imagine that] because of their [renewed] attachment to Him, God gives them the idea to leave their city to pray to God. Then, precisely on the day they decide to leave, the river suddenly swelled... and flooded the whole city. In this scenario, God's decree [to flood the city] was never repealed, and yet He saved them.*

Or picture the ministering angles [acting] on a set course — like horses running on a track. They do not run in order to be good or bad; it is simply the way of horses to run on a course. Now imagine that there is a blind man standing on the racetrack. [Because of his handicap,] he does not know how horses behave — whether they will go toward the right or toward the left — so he has no choice but to rely on the protection of someone who can see and does know their habits. Then the [horses came] running on one side [of the track] and the [seeing person] led the blind person [out of their way] to the other side. The horses did not change their course, yet the blind person was saved. [Similarly, the angels function on a set course, yet God can "pull" the righteous out of their way.]

Therefore after the Torah notes that "Hashem, your God, has apportioned [the heavenly bodies] to all the peoples," (Devarim 4:19), it continues with the one exception: "But Hashem has taken you and withdrawn you from the iron furnace... to be a nation of heritage for Him...." (ibid. v. 20). "Unlike these is the Portion of Jacob, for He is the Molder of everything, and Israel is the tribe that is His heritage..." (Yirmiyah 10:16). This is also the meaning of our Sages' saying (Shabbos 156a): "There is no mazal for Israel" ("Israel's fate is not controlled by the stars") — as long as they keep the Torah. However, if they do not keep it then the mazal can control them....

Indeed, the array [of the constellations] indicated that [the Jews] were destined to remain in the exile of Egypt for many more years, but because they cried out to Hashem and they returned to Him, God saved them. This [special protection] is extended not only to the public but also to individuals. How fortunate, then, are those who keep the Torah!

— Ibn Ezra, Commentary to Shemos 33:21

I. When hidden miracles become open miracles

As we have seen, "hidden" miracles are only hidden in the sense that God's involvement in those events was concealed in nature. But when God's hand is seen in natural events, then they too become "open" miracles. The primary example of hidden miracles becoming open ones is when they are done for many people all at the same time. That is, when the Jewish people as a whole enjoy unprecedented blessing, it becomes obvious that it was God's doing. The Ramban points this out in his commentary to *Vayikra* (26:11):

> *These blessings, which are many and [are addressed to the] general [community] — such as rain, plentitude, peace and the fruitfulness of people — are not the same brief blessings He had bestowed earlier, saying (Shemos 23:25), "and He will bless your food and your drink; and I will eliminate [any] illness from among you." There he assured us that we would have food and drink, which would be a blessing for us, preventing sickness to our bodies. Consequently, the organs of procreation will be complete and healthy, we will give birth properly, and we will live full lives, as He said (ibid. v. 26), "There will be no woman who miscarries or is childless in your land. I will grant you your full number of years." Likewise, at the beginning [of that set of blessings], He said (ibid. 15:26), "for I am Hashem your Healer."*
>
> *The reason for this [division of the blessings into two sections] is that although all the blessings [mentioned in the Torah] are miraculous, yet they are hidden miracles (of which the whole Torah is full, as I have explained).*[3] *[Blessings] can apply even to an individual who serves [Him], for when a pious man keeps all the commandments of his God, the Eternal God guards him from sickness,*

3. In his commentary to *Shemos* 13:16, quoted above, section A.

barreness and bereavement, and he will live out his days in goodness. The blessings stated in this section, however, are general ones that apply to the people as a whole and only [take effect] when the whole of our people are righteous. This is why in this section it always emphasizes the land: "and the land shall yield" (Vayikra 26:4); "in your land safely" (v. 5); "peace in the land… out of the land… no armed forces will go through your land" (v. 6) — [because these blessings are addressed to the nation as a whole, when they dwell "in the land"].

Now, we have already explained that all these blessings are miracles, for it is not natural that rainfall should be dependent on our observing the statutes and commandments of God, or that [observance] would give us peace from our enemies while making them so faint-hearted that a hundred of them would flee before five of us. [Nor is it natural] for the opposite to occur because of our planting in the Seventh year.

But although they are hidden miracles, for they are [brought about] by natural means and follow standard patterns of nature, yet [the Torah mentions them separately because] these events come to be known [as miracles] because of their constant and continuous occurrences in the whole land. If one righteous man lives, and God takes away sickness from him, and he lives out his days [it would not be acknowledged as miraculous], for this also happens to some wicked people. But when an entire land and a whole people always have rain in the right season; and they have plentitude, security, peace, health, and strength; and they achieve victory over their enemies — in a manner unmatched anywhere in the whole world — it becomes known to all that "this is Hashem's doing" (Tehillim 118:23). Therefore, He said, "And all the nations of the earth will see that Hashem's Name is displayed upon you, and they will be afraid of you" (Devarim 28:10).

Not only through blessings can God be seen but also through curses can He be seen. The Ramban goes on to say that if the Jews, Heaven forbid, transgress the commandments, then too their affairs "are not conducted at all by the natural order of things":

> *Or, the opposite can occur, as a result of the curses, if punishments come upon the land — such as, "And I will make your heaven as iron" (Vayikra 26:19), and punishments of sickness, as He said (Devarim 28:59), "severe and chronic illnesses," meaning that the food will be spoiled and bring about sickness, and thus the miracle will be made known to all because of its continued existence amongst the whole people. There it is written (ibid. 29:21), "Then, when the later generation — your children who arise from those [who come] after you — and the gentile who comes from a distant land, see the plagues of that land, and the afflictions, they will say...." They will not wonder at that [single] man upon whom "the entire curse that is written in this Book will be brought to bear against him" (ibid. v. 19), for it happens many times in the natural order of the world, among all nations, that bad happenings come upon certain individuals. It is only with reference to "that land" that the nations wonder, "Why did Hashem do such a thing to this land?" (ibid. v. 23) because everyone will see and understand "that the hand of Hashem has done this" (Yeshayah 41:20). And [the reason for the calamities will also be obvious to them], and they will say, "Because they abandoned the covenant of Hashem, the God of their forefathers" (Devarim 29:24).*
>
> — *Vayikra 26:11*

J. When Israel is on the ultimate level

On the ultimate level, the Ramban teaches, when the Jews serve God at the peak of observance, then everything that happens to them is miraculous, by the hand of God:

In general, then, when Israel is perfect, constituting a large number, their affairs are not conducted at all by the natural order of things — neither themselves nor their land, neither collectively nor individually — for God blesses their bread and their water.

— Ramban, Commentary to Vayikra 26:11

CHAPTER NINE

Belief in Special Providence

A. How is belief in hidden miracles the foundation of the Torah?

We have been discussing the significance of hidden miracles, which — as the Ramban wrote — "constitute the foundation of the whole Torah" (*Ramban, Shemos* 13:16). These words of the Ramban are perplexing: Why should a lack of belief in hidden miracles make a person a heretic? If someone believes in all the other principles of faith, in the Divine origin of the Torah, and in the importance of the mitzvos, and the only matter in which he lacks faith is the existence of hidden miracles — why should he be considered as one that "has no part in the entire Torah"?

Briefly, the answer is: because the aim and purpose of the entire Torah is to help us "find" God in the world. He is "hiding" in nature, and our task is to see Him by looking for instances of specific providence and hidden miracles. When we hone our faith, it becomes obvious to us that it is He Who is conducting the world.

In fact, all the principles of faith, all the mitzvos, and all the Torah's words are directed at this aim. For the true issue here is faith. To Jews, human perfection is measured by the intensity of one's faith, for it is the measure of one's closeness to God. And the closer a person is to God, the closer God is to the person: He watches over him more closely and He bestows more of His good upon him. In this regard, then, we can say that faith is the root of all life. It is thus quite appropriate to call faith and belief in hidden miracles "the foundation of the whole Torah." Someone who lacks this is indeed missing the entire point of the Torah. Perhaps a good parable for this concept is the life of a human being. All the parts of a person — his flesh, limbs, organs, blood, mind, and heart and all his faculties — are directed to one purpose: to be a living person. Yet, even if a person possesses all of these "ingredients" but is missing the main one, "life," we would not say that he has everything, and he is "only" missing life. Rather, we would say he is not a live human! Likewise, knowing God is the source of life: "The righteous person shall live through his faith" (*Chavakkuk* 2:4)!

We will devote the rest of this chapter to expanding and explaining this answer.

B. Seeing God in this world

According to the above, belief in hidden miracles is actually the ability to see God in the world. Once we know that fact, we can see that the Torah often refers to this concept, though it uses various terms to do so. The duties of the heart — such as, knowing God, faith, awe, love, and attachment — are all connected to this central idea, as we shall see. Knowledge of God is the firm awareness of the fundamentals of faith, mainly the knowledge of God's providence. This is the significance of the verses: "You shall realize [it] today and impress [it] upon your heart, that it is Hashem Who is God in Heaven above and on the earth below; there is none other" (*Devarim* 4:39); "So that all the peoples of the earth shall know that Hashem is God — there is no other" (*I Melachim* 8:60); "For only with this may one glorify himself – contemplating and knowing Me, for I am Hashem Who does kindness, justice and righteousness in the land, for in these is My desire — the word of Hashem" (*Yirmiyah* 9:23); "Know the God of your father and serve Him" (*I Divrei HaYamim* 28:9).

Faith is a tangible, firm belief in God that resides in the person's heart, as in: "Impress [it] upon your heart" (*Devarim* 4:39).

Awe is the feeling of submission and fear of God felt by all the emotions — it is the feeling of standing in His presence.

Love is the great admiration a person feels when he recognizes all the good that God has extended to him. The person then feels a desire to "give back" something, so he tries doing only acts that will be pleasing to God.

Attachment is having the above mentioned understanding, knowledge, etc. on one's mind constantly, without any interruption by any physical matter or needs of the body. Once a person has trained all his limbs and faculties to submit completely to God's will, he becomes "tied" and "connected" to Him by God's "light" that dwells upon him. This is the highest, most perfect state of insight of God possible for man.

C. The purpose of creation is for knowing God

The Rambam (in his introduction to the Order of *Zeraim* in the Mishnah) writes:

> *Know that the ancients devoted much contemplation [into the meaning of life] — as they were blessed with superior wisdom and intellect — and concluded that everything that exists must have some purpose that justifies its exis-*

tence.... Man, they found..., has only one true purpose, and it was only for that reason that he was created. All his other activities, however, are merely to sustain his life so that he will be able to fulfill that one purpose. That one task is: to formulate deep thoughts in his soul and to know Truth as such. For common sense tells us that it is a lie and falsehood [to claim] that the purpose of man is simply to eat, drink, and procreate, or to build [palaces] — for these are all [extrinsic] occurrences that arise from time to time; they do not add anything to man's inner value. Besides, he shares these [activities] with most creatures, [so they cannot be what set him apart from other creatures]. However, it is wisdom that adds inner value [to man] and that can transform [a person] from a contemptible level to one of respect. For [without wisdom] a person is only a "man" in potential, but [with it] he becomes a man in actuality. A human that does not think and has no comprehension is like an animal, for the only difference between [a human] and any other type of beast is his ability to think. And the most noble thoughts are those that are used to contemplate the unity of the Holy One, Blessed is He, and other aspects of God [that directly give us insight to how God conducts the world]. For all other branches of wisdom are only necessary to [help man] sharpen [his mind] until he is ready to know Godly wisdom.

— Rambam, Introduction to Zeraim

Rabbi Shmuel Ibn Tibon, the great translator of the Rambam's works, writes (in his introduction to the Rambam's *Shemonah Perakim*) that "Knowing God is undoubtedly the purpose of man, as the prophet says, 'For only with this may one glorify himself – contemplating and knowing Me, for I am Hashem Who does kindness, justice and righteousness in the land, for in these is My desire — the word of Hashem' "(*Yirmiyah* 9:23). The verse quoted is discussing the idea of God's providence and His deeds on earth. From the context of the verse, then, we see that acknowledging God's providence is called "knowing" God, and this awareness is the purpose of man. (See there further, and see *Moreh Nevuchim* III:51.)

D. The Torah helps us see God

The aim of the Torah, as well, is to assist us to "see" God, as the Ramban writes (*Commentary* to *Shemos* 13:16): "The purpose of all the commandments is that we should come to believe in our God, and acknowledge to Him that He created us." Another source that clearly shows the importance of coming to know God (in the sense of acknowledging that God created and continues to conduct the world) is the Rambam we discussed earlier, in Chapter Four. The Rambam described at length how Avraham Avinu publicized God's Name in the world, and how this tradition was continued by Yitzchak and Yaakov and the tribes. He then writes:

> *[This pattern] continued and intensified among the children of Yaakov and among those who accompanied them; and thus a nation who knew of God was formed in the world. But after the Jews had been in Egypt for many days, they learned to act like [the Egyptians] and worship stars like them. The only exception was the tribe of Levi.... At any moment the root that Avraham planted was about to be uprooted, and the children of Yaakov were about to [completely] revert to the world's errors and wayward behavior. Yet because of God's love for us and because He kept the oath that He swore to our forefather Avraham (see Devarim 7:8), He prepared and sent Moshe Rabbeinu, the master of all the prophets [to save them].*
>
> *Rambam, Hilchos Akum, Ch. 1*

One straightforward example of how the mitzvos accomplish this goal is the mitzvah of *mezuzah*:

> *A person must be very careful [in the mitzvah] of mezuzah because it is an obligation upon everyone at all times. Whenever a person enters or leaves [his home] he will*

encounter the unity of Hashem, the Name of the Holy One, and he will remember the love of Him. He will then awaken from his slumber and preoccupation with the vanities of time. And he will know that the only everlasting thing is the knowledge of the Rock of the world.
— Rambam, Hilchos Mezuzah 6:13

E. Behavior affects awareness

The Rambam writes in *Hilchos Teshuvah*:

> *The Holy One gave us this Torah, it is the Tree of Life, and whoever does all that is written in it and knows it completely and thoroughly, will thereby merit life in the World to Come. The extent of one's merit depends on the greatness of his deeds and the scope of his knowledge.*
> *— Rambam, Hilchos Teshuvah 9:1*

How do good deeds and Torah knowledge create merit? The answer is that, as we have seen, the purpose of studying the Torah is for the sake of "knowing God," and knowing God is its own best reward. Likewise, keeping the mitzvos of the Torah also has this effect for they embody the Torah's wisdom. Thus it is written, "[There is] good understanding to all those who practice it" (*Tehillim* 111:10).

For deeper insight into this concept, let us turn to another passage written by the Rambam, in *Moreh Nevuchim*:

> *We do not sit, move, and occupy ourselves when we are alone and at home, in the same manner as we do in the presence of a great king; we speak and open our mouth as we please when we are with the people of our own household and with our relatives, but not so when we are in a royal assembly. If we therefore desire to attain human perfection, and to be truly men of God, we must awake from our sleep, and bear in mind that the great King that is over us, and is always joined to us, is greater than any earthly king, greater than David and Solomon. The King*

that cleaves to us and embraces us is the intellect that influences us, and forms the link between us and God. Just as we perceive God by means of the light that He sends down upon us (as the verse states, "By Your light may we see light" [Tehillim 36:9]) so too, does God look down upon us through that same light. Indeed, because of [that light] He is always with us, watching and seeing: "Can a man hide in concealed places that I would not see him? (Yirmiyah 23:24). Devote much thought to this.

When the perfect bear this in mind, they are filled with awe, subservience, and fear of God; their reverence and shame before God is truthful — not illusory — in such a manner that their conduct, even when alone with their wives or in the bath, will be as modest as it is in public interactions with other people.... You know also how much [the Sages] warned us not to walk arrogantly upright since "the whole world is filled with His glory" (Yeshayah 6:3). [They instructed us to] behave this way so that the above-mentioned idea will be firmly established in the hearts of men; namely, that we are always in God's hands, and it is in the presence of His glory that we come and go.

— Moreh Nevuchim III:52

If we carefully study what the Rambam has written here, we will notice that there is two-way relationship between action and awareness of God: the more aware we are of being in God's presence, the more we behave contritely etc.; and the more we behave appropriately, the more it reminds us that we are in His presence. This relationship certainly applies to the mitzvos of the Torah, as the Rambam continues with in the next paragraph.

F. Love of God comes fromTorah study; fear of God comes from doing its mitzvos

What I have pointed out here to you is the object of all deeds of the Torah. For by [carrying out] all the details of those prescribed practices, and repeating them continually, some pious men become accustomed [to them] and attain human perfection. They then fear God and revere Him; they know Who is with them, so they do [only] what is proper. God has made it clear that the object of all the deeds of the Torah is to lead man to... fear God and to revere His word, for He said, "If you are not careful to do all the words of this Torah that are written in this Book, so as to fear this glorified and fearful Name, Hashem, your God..." (Devarim 28:58). Consider how He made it clear to us that the only object and aim of "all the words of this Torah" is to [make man] "fear the glorified and fearful Name." That this end is attained by certain acts we likewise learn from the phrase employed in this verse: "If you are not careful to do... so as to fear." [This phrase] clearly shows that [fear of God] is attained [by doing] actions, which are the positive and the negative [precepts]. But the truths that the Torah teaches us — the knowledge of God's existence and His unity — teach us to love God.... The two objects, love and fear of God, are acquired by two different means. The love is the result of the truths of the Torah, which includes the true knowledge of the existence of God; while fear of God is produced by the practices prescribed in the Law. Consider this explanation.

— Rambam, Moreh Nevuchim III:52

We can now re-examine the passage from *Hilchos Teshuvah*: The Rambam there writes that there are two requirements for meriting life in the World to Come: knowing the Torah thoroughly and doing all that is written in it. In light of the Rambam's comments in *Moreh Nevuchim*, when he wrote (in *Hilchos Teshuvah*) "whoever does all that is written in it," he was referring to the "deeds of the Torah," which allow the person to acquire awe of God; and the requirement of "and knows it completely and thoroughly" refers to the "truths of the Torah," which instill within a person love of God. These two obligations — which can only stem from a firm belief in God's providence — are the purpose of the entire Torah!

It is no wonder, then, that if someone both studies the Torah and actively keeps its mitzvos, he "will thereby merit life in the World to Come."

G. The providence that comes from being attached to God

Earlier, in section A, we posited that the stronger one's faith, the closer he is to God, and "the closer a person is to God, the closer God is to the person." This point, as well, was made by the Rambam quoted above:

> *Just as we perceive God by means of the light that He sends down upon us (as the verse states, "By Your light may we see light" [Tehillim 36:9]) so too, does God look down upon us through that same light.*
> — *Moreh Nevuchim III:52*

However, the Rambam discussed this much more at length in the preceding chapter of *Moreh Nevuchim* (III:51), an excerpt of which follows:

> *I have shown to you that the intellect, which emanates from God unto us, is the link that joins us to Him. You have it in your power [through free will] to strengthen that bond, if you choose to do so, or to weaken it gradually until it breaks, if you prefer this. It will only become strong when you employ it in the love of God, and seek that love; it will be weakened when you direct your thoughts to other things. You must know that even if you were the wisest man in respect to the true knowledge of God, you break the bond between you and God whenever you turn your thoughts entirely to the necessary food or any necessary business; you are then not with God, and He is not with you, for that relation between you and Him is actually interrupted in those moments. The pious were therefore particular to restrict the time in which they could not meditate upon the Name [of God] saying, "Do not*

vacate God from your thoughts" (Shabbos 149a). Similarly, David said, "I have set Hashem before me always; because He is at my right hand I shall not falter" (Tehillim 16:8). That is, [David was saying that] I do not turn my thoughts away from God, for He is like my right hand, which I never forget — not even for a moment — on account of the ease of its motions, and therefore "I shall not falter"....

A wonderful thought came to me, one that can remove many doubts and explain Divine mysteries. We have already stated in the chapters which treat of Divine providence, that providence watches over every rational being according to the amount of intellect which that being possesses. Those who are perfect in their perception of God, whose minds are never separated from Him, enjoy special providence constantly. But those who are perfect in their knowledge of God yet sometimes turn their mind away from God, enjoy the presence of Divine providence only when they meditate on God — but when their thoughts are engaged in other matters, Divine providence departs from them. The absence of providence in this case is not like its absence in the case of those who do not reflect on God at all; rather, it is merely less intense [than what he usually enjoys]....

Hence, it appears to me that whenever [ordinary] evils befall a prophet or a perfectly pious man, it is only at such moments of distraction. Furthermore, the intensity of the evil is proportional to the duration of those moments, or to the character of the things that occupies their mind....

If man frees his thoughts from worldly matters, obtains a knowledge of God in this right way, and rejoices in that knowledge, it is impossible that any kind of evil should befall him, for he is with God, and God with him. But when he takes his mind off God, when he is separated from God, then God is also separated from him; and then he is exposed to any evil that might befall him....

I found that this principle is also expressed in the Torah: "I will... hide My Face from them, [that] they will be for plunder, and many misfortunes and calamities will befall them. And on that day they will say, 'Is it not because our God is not among us, that these misfortunes have befallen us?'" (Devarim 31:17). It is clear that we are the cause of this "hiding of the Face" [when God acts as though He is oblivious of us], and that we are the ones who create the screen that separates us from God. It is therefore said, "And I will surely hide My face on that day, because of all the evil that they have done" (ibid. v. 18). In this regard, there is undoubtedly no difference between one single person and a whole community; [in both cases the gift of being protected by God is dependent on being attached to Him].

It should now be clear to you that the cause for some individuals being exposed to chance or being abandoned to destruction like cattle, is their separation from God. But those who have God dwelling in [their hearts], are not touched by any evil whatsoever. For God says, "Fear not, for I am with you; be not dismayed, for I am your God" (Yeshayah 41:10).... For anybody who perfects himself such that the [Divine] Intellect flows upon him becomes attached to Divine providence and all the evils of the world are held away from him.

Moreh Nevuchim III:51

H. Torah is light

In Chapter One we learned that not only did God create the word in the six days of creation but also He still supports and conducts it. Everything that exists — whether small or large — is reactivated every instant by God Himself. He did not abandon the world to the control of the ministering angels. He alone supervises everything and rules over everything.

There are two systems by which He operates the world: either by general (natural) providence or by special (miraculous) providence. Which system will be used for a particular individual depends on that person's deeds and merits — in other words, on the choices he makes. In order for someone to merit God's special providence, he must get close and attach himself to the Source that created, and continues to conduct, everything.

What "flows" from this Source? It is the Supreme Intelligence that emanates from Him. Thus the *Targum Yerushalmi* (*Bereishis* 1:1) renders the first verse of the Torah, "God created [the world] with wisdom." The Commentary to *Targum Yerushalmi* explains, "That is, by means of the Supreme Intelligence."

In *Mishlei* (3:19-20) it is written, "Hashem founded the earth with wisdom; He established the heavens with understanding; through His knowledge, the depths were cleaved." These verses allude to the three types of wisdom that were used in the creation of the world: wisdom, understanding, and knowledge. These are the very qualities that Betzalel, the chief builder of the Mishkan, used to construct the Mishkan. The Midrash (*Shemos Rabbah* 48:4) explains the significance of each:

> *["I have endowed him with a Divine spirit, with wisdom, understanding, and knowledge, and with the skill of every craft" (Shemos 31:3).] With wisdom — that he was wise in Torah; with ... understanding — that he understood Halachah; and with knowledge — that he had complete knowledge of Talmud.*
>
> — *Shemos Rabbah 48:4*

If we apply these definitions of wisdom, understanding and knowledge to the verse in *Mishlei*, then it can be understood as saying that God created the world "with Torah, Halachah, and Talmud." Thus, not only was the Torah God's "blueprint" of the world (see *Zohar, Terumah*, p. 161b: "He looked in the Torah and created the world") but also His "tools" with which He created it. Our Sages showed this from a verse in *Mishlei* (9:1): "'With all forms of wisdom did she build her house' — this is the Torah that built the whole world with its wisdom" (*Yalkut Shimoni, Mishlei* §944). Rabbi Chaim of Volozhin, in *Nefesh HaChaim* (IV:10), quotes and elaborates on this Midrash. He explains that God's "light" with which He created (and continues to sustain) the world is actually the Torah. That the Torah is called light we see from *Mishlei* (6:23): "For a commandment is a lamp and the Torah is light."

Once we have established that the world is sustained only by God's light and that this light is the Torah, then we can begin to appreciate why Torah study is so important:

> *Therefore, the life, light, and very survival of all the worlds only exists when we properly toil in [Torah study] — for "the Holy One, the Torah, and Israel are all one" (see Zohar, Acharei 73a).*
>
> — *Nefesh HaChaim IV:11*

Accordingly, when the Torah says that God created the world "*Bereishis*" ("In the beginning") it can be read literally: God created the world "with the beginning, which is the Torah, as Rashi to (*Bereishis* 1:1) shows: "[God created the world] for the sake of the Torah, which is called 'the beginning of His way' (*Mishlei* 8:22), and for the sake of Israel who are called 'the beginning of His crop'" (*Yirmiyah* 2:3).

From the Rambam's comments regarding the verse, "By Your light may we see light" (*Tehillim* 36:10), we can infer that in order for man to have faith and knowledge of the Creator, his heart and mind must receive the flow of God's light. Since the main way a person attains this light is by studying the Torah, it follows that somebody who sincerely studies the Torah thereby attains ever-higher levels of faith.

The Rambam, quoted above, writes that "Those who are perfect in their perception of God, whose minds are never separated from Him, enjoy special providence constantly." In the context of our discussion, this means that someone who is constantly engaged in Torah study deserves extra providence. With this thought in mind, Rashi's comment on the beginning of *Parshas Bechukosai* (*Vayikra* 26:3) becomes almost self-explanatory. The Torah portion of *Bechukosai* discusses the Blessings and Curses reserved for those who follow or disobey the Torah. The portion begins with, "If you pursue My statutes, and keep My commandments and do them, I will provide your rains at their time, the land will yield its produce." Thus, the Torah promises blessing — for this world and the next — only on condition that "you pursue My statues." Rashi, based on the Midrash, comments: "If you pursue My statutes — If you will toil in the study of the Torah." As we noted above, special providence depends on our minds being focused on God, which is done by constant Torah study. Conversely, "If you do not listen to me" (ibid v. 14) means "if you do not toil in the Torah" you will eventually deny the essential of faith and you will suffer the consequences of all the curses listed there.

Similarly, in the paragraph of *Ve'haya im shamo'a* (*Devarim* 11:15-16) — which outlines the obligation to accept the yolk of Heaven, the Torah, and the mitzvos — the Torah warns us, "You will eat and be satisfied. Be careful that your hearts do not entice [you], and you go astray and serve estranged gods." Rashi explains:

> *Once you have eaten and are full, take heed that you do not kick [against God]; for no man rebels against the Holy One, Blessed is He, except out of satiety.... "And you go astray" — to depart from the Torah, for through this "you will serve other gods," because as soon as a man departs from the Torah he goes and clings to idol worship. David similarly said, "for they have driven me away this day from attaching myself to the heritage of Hashem, [as if] to say, 'Go worship the gods of others!'" (I Shmuel 26:19). Did anyone [really] say this to him? However, [he meant]: Since I have been driven away from occupying myself with the Torah, I am more susceptible to serving other gods.*
>
> *— Rashi to Devarim 11:15-16*

This is yet another example where we see that the intensity of one's faith depends on the effort the person invests in studying the Torah, for the Holy One, the Torah, and Israel are one. "In Your light may we see light"!

I. The power of action

However, God also decreed that, in addition to studying the Torah, man must also do actions if he truly wishes to attain the position of deep faith. Thus it is written, "[There is] good understanding to all those that practice it" (*Tehillim* 111:10). The need to do physical actions of faith alongside intellectual study arises from the fact that man is a composite of body and soul. Because of the way man was created, wisdom only fully penetrates his being through certain physical actions. Actions, then, have the power to engrave wisdom upon man. This is the significance of "mitzvos of action," which we will discuss in detail in the next chapter.

CHAPTER TEN

Faith and Mitzvos

A. The importance of action in mitzvos

A consummate Jew both learns the Torah and actively performs the mitzvos. He knows that one without the other is insufficient. The Torah and the commandments are obviously connected to each other, but what is that relationship? King Shlomo enlightened us in this matter: "For a commandment is a lamp and the Torah is light" (*Mishlei* 6:23). All lighting devices are made of two parts: the lamp, which is the container for the fuel and the wick; and the light, which is the flame. One without the other cannot work: a flame that is not contained in a lamp does not illuminate — it consumes and quickly becomes extinguished;

and a lamp without the flame certainly does not illuminate — it stagnates and remains lifeless. That, says King Shlomo, is the relationship between the Torah and the mitzvos: the "light" is the Torah, and the "containers" for that light are the practiced mitzvos. One without the other cannot work: "Anyone whose good deeds exceed his wisdom, his wisdom will endure; but anyone whose wisdom exceeds his good deeds, his wisdom will not endure" (*Avos* 3:12).

The *Sefer HaChinuch* explains why mitzvos that require action are so important:

> *And now, my son, if [you seek] understanding, listen to this;*[1] *incline your ear and hear*[2] *— I will instruct you for your benefit*[3] *regarding Torah and mitzvos. Know that people are influenced by their movements, and their thoughts and feelings always follow their actions — whether for good or for bad. Even someone who is thoroughly wicked and all day his heart thinks only of evil,*[4] *still if he pours out his soul and dedicates his efforts to consistently engage in Torah and mitzvos, then — even if he does this not for the sake of Heaven — he is guaranteed to turn to the good. "By [doing them for] unworthy motives [one can] come [to do them] for worthy motives" (Pesachim 50b). With the power of one's actions, a person can kill his evil inclination, for the hearts of people follow their movements. Conversely, even if someone is completely righteous, but for some reason is constantly involved in negative matters (such as if a king forcefully appointed him to an evil occupation), then his righteous heart will eventually be transformed into a completely evil one. Again, the reason for this is that people are influenced by their movements, as we have said. This is why our Sages said that "The Holy One,*

1. Cf. *Iyov* 34:16.
2. Cf. *Yeshaya* 37:17.
3. Cf. ibid. 48:17.
4. Cf. *Bereishis* 6:5.

Blessed is He, wished to confer merit upon Israel; therefore He gave them Torah and mitzvos in abundance" (Mishnah Makkos 3:16), for He wants our thoughts to be completely occupied with them, and all of our affairs to revolve around them — in order to give us good in our end. For through good actions we are influenced to be good and we thereby merit everlasting life.
— *Sefer HaChinuch §16*

B. Physical actions for the physical body

How are actions so influential? The answer lies in the fact that a human being is made of two parts: body and soul, matter and spirit. The reason man was created this way was to give him free will (which can only operate when there are choices), but a consequence of this duality is that the Torah, which is a spiritual entity, does not have as much influence on the body as do physical actions. For this reason, mitzvos that require physical action have great influence on the body.

We can now appreciate God's command to keep 248 positive mitzvos — giving us a mitzvah for each of our 248 limbs and organs (this idea is discussed at length in *Sefer Chareidim*). Through these commandments, God sanctified us, and each mitzvah we do brings upon us an abundance of light that emanates from His holiness, so to speak. This has a profound influence upon us, for it reveals some of His glory to us and it connects us to Him, giving us life. Thus it is written, "But you, who adhere to Hashem, are all living today" (*Devarim* 4:4).

C. "Feeding" faith

This Divine influence that flows upon us when we keep both the Torah and the mitzvos was referred to as "Divine enlightenment" (*ha'sechel ha'Eloki*) by the Rambam, the Kuzari, and others; or as "a spirit of holiness" (*ruach kedushah*) by the Kabbalists (such as in *Sefer HaKedushah*, by Rabbi Chaim Vital). Both terms, however, refer to the spiritual effect on the individual. As we saw above, even if we study Torah and contemplate matters of faith, if we do not take actions that enable us to live in a state of faith (i.e. if we have the "light" but lack the "lamp") then our enlightenment will not endure. At most, we will have achieved an intellectual recognition of God, but it will still fall short of true, lasting faith.

To make our "enlightenment" or "spirit" last, we must keep physical mitzvos alongside contemplating God's wisdom. This is the only way to come to true faith — as is written, "The beginning of wisdom is fear of Hashem" (*Tehillim* 111:10). If we wish to sustain our faith, then we must "feed it" constantly with Torah and mitzvos — for they are its "food." Just as one's body cannot thrive without its food, so too, one's faith cannot thrive without its food — "All Your commandments are faith" (ibid. 119:86)!

We can see this link between keeping the Torah and mitzvos and firm faith in the story of Amalek's war against Israel. The Torah tells us that "Amalek then came and fought with Israel at Refidim" (*Shemos* 17:8). The Sages explain that the reason Amalek was allowed to approach Israel was because Israel "loosened their hand (*rafu yedeihem*) from [gripping] the Torah" (*Yalkut Shimoni, Yisro* §263). This explanation seems to contradict the reason the Torah itself gives, for the verse says that Israel's shortcoming was that they lacked faith, for they asked: "Is Hashem among us or not?" (*Shemos* 17:7). However, in light of our discussion, the two explanations complement each other: The reason their faith became weak was that they were lax in keeping the Torah and the mitzvos.

Thus, laxity in Torah and mitzvos leads directly to weakening faith; but by fulfilling the Torah, faith is generated and intensified. This is especially true when one is constantly engaged in Torah study, for "the study of Torah is equivalent to them all" (*Mishnah Pe'ah* 1:1).

In Chapter Fourteen we will discuss the question of how one's deeds can exceed his wisdom — how can someone do more than he knows?

CHAPTER ELEVEN

From Exodus to Revelation

A. Faith from the Revelation at Sinai

Now that we have established that the Exodus from Egypt is our main source of faith in God and His power, we may be troubled with a difficult question. The Rambam, in his discussion of Moshe Rabbeinu, explains why we believe in Moshe's prophecy:

> *Israel did not believe in Moshe Rabbeinu because of the miracles he performed, for whoever believes because of miracles is doubtful: perhaps the sign was done through sorcery or magic. The miracles that Moshe did in the desert were*

all done out of necessity, not as proof for his prophecy. For instance, it was necessary to drown the Egyptians, so he split the Sea and caused them to sink in it. We needed food, so he brought down manna ....

But what, then, led them to believe in him? The Revelation at Mount Sinai. For we saw and heard for ourselves the sounds, the fire, and the torches as he approached the fog. [We heard] the voice say: "Moshe, Moshe, go and tell them such-and-such," as the verse says, "Face to face Hashem spoke with you" (Devarim 5:4).

— Rambam, Hilchos Yesodei HaTorah 8:1

The Rambam's point is that the wonder of the Revelation at Mount Sinai was far more spectacular and convincing than all the miracles of the Exodus. Therefore, although the Rambam's topic was Moshe's prophecy, we may still infer that our faith in God should also come mainly from the Revelation, not the Exodus. In fact, the Rambam elsewhere does seem to imply that the Revelation is the strongest source for faith:

It behooves you, our brothers, to raise your children [with the knowledge] of that momentous event; you should publicly recount His greatness and Majesty — for [the Revelation at Sinai] is the pillar upon which [our] faith stands, and the argument that leads to the Truth. Elevate that event above all other events, as God did.

— Rambam, The Letter to Yemen

Why, then, is the Exodus considered the main source of our faith?

B. The Revelation was the culmination of the Exodus

The answer is: neither the Exodus nor the Revelation is our "main" source of faith; rather, they complement each other. When the Rambam wrote that the Jews did not believe in Moshe because of the miracles he performed, "for whoever believes because of miracles is doubtful," he meant that, on their own, miracles leave room for doubt. But once the Jews also experienced the Revelation, and they witnessed God communicating with Moshe, they were convinced that not only is he a true prophet but that all the miracles he had predicted until then were truly acts of God. Whatever doubts they had had at first were resolved with the Revelation. It became clear to them that it was God "Who caused His splendrous arm to go at Moshe's right side" (*Yeshayah* 63:12). Thus, together with the Revelation, the miracles of the Exodus are potent sources for our faith, as the Rambam explicitly states:

> *The Holy One informed [Moshe that] these signs are intended [to prove his legitimacy] only until they would leave Egypt, but once they would leave and they would stand at [Mount Sinai], "Whatever doubts they have about you will vanish."*
> *— Rambam, Hilchos Yesodei HaTorah 8:2*

Still, we may wonder, what is the benefit of recalling the miracles of the Exodus now that we have experienced the clarity of the Revelation? What could be more proof than the Revelation ?

> *When the Holy One, Blessed is He, gave the Torah, He opened the seven heavens for them. And just as He parted the higher regions so did He part the lower ones, so that they saw that He was the sole [God]. This is why it is stated, "You have been shown in order to know that Hashem, He is the God. There is none beside Him!"*
> *— Rashi, Devarim 4:35*

Furthermore, the Revelation was a prophetic experience — one that leaves no room for doubt — so what is the significance of the Exodus with regard to faith?

The miracles of the Exodus, however, had one advantage over the Revelation at Sinai. True, the Revelation was an overwhelming, prophetic experience, but it happened as a single event, over a relatively short time. The miracles of the Exodus, on the other hand, were numerous and occurred over a span of many months. Because of man's physical nature, the only impressions that endure are those that the person experiences repeatedly. The Jews, therefore, needed detailed object lessons (that touched on all aspects of the natural world, as we saw above in Chapters Six and Seven) that would be repeated until they would permeate the Jews' entire being. Hence, the Revelation gave the Jews clarity in their faith, but the Exodus is what guaranteed its permanence. The plain reading of Scripture conveys this very point:

> *Ask now about earlier times that were before you, from the day that God created man on earth, and [ask every being that exists] from one end of the heavens to the other: Was there ever anything like this great thing, or was something like it ever heard of? Did [another] people hear the voice of God speaking from within the fire as you heard it, and remain alive?! Or did any god perform such miracles to come and take for himself one nation from the midst of [another] nation, with trials, signs, wonders and battle, with mighty force, extended power and great manifestations, like everything Hashem, your God, did for you in Egypt before your eyes? You have been shown in order to know that Hashem, He is the God. There is none beside Him!"*
> — *Devarim 4:32-36*

These verses imply that they were "shown" the Revelation and the Exodus "in order to know that Hashem, He is the God. There is none beside Him." (This is also how the Ramban seems to have understood these verses.)

The *Sefer HaChinuch*, in fact, incorporates both the Exodus and the Revelation into the one general concept of faith:

> *The commandment to believe in the existence of God: To believe that the world has one God Who created everything that exists; and that everything that is, was, and will ever be — comes from His power and will. [We are also to believe] that it was He Who took us out of Egypt and gave us the Torah, as is written at the outset of the giving of the*

Torah, "I am Hashem, your God, Who took you out of the land of Egypt ..." (Shemos 20:2); which means, "Know and believe that the world has a God," for the word Anochi, "I am," indicates that [I] exist. Then, when the verse continues, "Who took you out of the land of Egypt ...," it is saying that you must not let your hearts mislead you to view your Exodus from Egypt and the Plagues of Egypt as mere coincidence; rather, know that "it is I Who took you out with [Divine] will and providence," as He had promised to Avraham, Yitzchak, and Yaakov.
— Sefer HaChinuch, Mitzvah 25

Yet another set of verses shows that the Revelation at Sinai was the culmination of the Exodus:

Say, therefore, to the Children of Israel, "I am Hashem. I will free you from the burdens of the Egyptians, release you from their servitude, and redeem you with extended power and great acts of judgment. I will take you as a nation for Me, and act as a God for you. You will recognize that it is I, Hashem, your God, Who is freeing you from the burdens of the Egyptians."
— Shemos 6:6-7

These verses are describing a sequence that begins with "I will free you," continues with "release ... and redeem," and concludes with "I will take you as a nation." The first three steps are the elements of the Exodus, but they lead to the giving of the Torah, as the Ibn Ezra (on that verse) writes, "'I will take you' — when you receive the Torah on Mount Sinai." Only then, after the Revelation, were they to "recognize that it is I, Hashem, your God, Who is freeing you from the burdens of the Egyptians."

C. True freedom

We may therefore say that our duty to remember the Exodus includes remembering the Revelation at Sinai and the giving of the Torah. This way of looking at the Revelation is supported by the fact that in the verses quoted above, the reference to the Revelation is the fourth term of redemption from Egypt. Accordingly, the four cups of wine we drink at the Seder (which correspond to these four terms of redemption) include one for the Revelation at Sinai!

On a deeper level, the Revelation was the culmination of the Exodus not only because it was the end of a process but also because it was only then that they were truly freed. In the words of the Ramban:

> *The exile was not completed until the day they returned to their place and to the status of their fathers. Although they had left Egypt and had made their way out of the house of bondage, they were still considered exiles because they were still in a land that was not theirs, stranded in the desert. But when they came to Mount Sinai and made the Mishkan, the Holy One caused His Divine Presence to dwell again amongst them. At last they returned to the status of their fathers, "when God's counsel was above their tent" (see Iyov 29:4), and they became the [bearers of God's glory in the world]. Then they were considered redeemed!*
>
> — *Ramban, Introduction to Shemos*

In fact, had Israel not sinned with the Golden Calf, the Revelation could have been the final redemption, because the Divine Presence had already come to dwell among them and they reached the level of supreme holiness, with the ability to communicate directly with God. But because of the Golden Calf, they forfeited their noble level.

Still, they were no longer in exile, for God continued to dwell among them, in the Mishkan, as the Ramban explains:

> *The secret of the Mishkan is that the Glory that [openly] dwelled upon Mount Sinai would now dwell upon it in a concealed manner.... Thus, Israel always had with them in the Mishkan the Glory that appeared to them on Mount Sinai. And when Moshe went into [the Mishkan], he*

would [hear] the same [type of] Utterance that was spoken to him at Mount Sinai. Thus just as it is said at the Giving of the Torah: "From Heaven He let you hear His Voice" (Devarim 4:36), so it is written of the Mishkan, "He heard the [Heavenly] Voice speaking with Itself for him [to hear], from above the cover... from between the two Cherubim; and [Hashem] spoke to him" (Bamidbar 7:89).
— Ramban, Shemos 25:1

D. Two events, two lessons

Another reason why we must recall both the miracles of the Exodus and the Revelation is that they reinforce two separate principles: The Exodus is the root of accepting the yoke of Heaven, while the Revelation at Mount Sinai is the root of faith, as we will see in Chapter Fourteen (We Will Do and We Will Listen).

CHAPTER TWELVE

The Revelation at Mount Sinai

Hashem then said to Moshe, "I am going to come to you in the thickness of the cloud, so that the people may hear when I speak with you, and they will also believe in you forever."

— Shemos 19:9

However, be careful and guard yourselves very well, so that you do not forget the things that your eyes saw, and that they are not removed from your heart your entire lifetime. Teach your children and grandchildren about the day you stood before Hashem, your God, at Chorev [Sinai], when Hashem said to me, "Assemble the people for Me and I will let them hear My words, so that they learn to fear Me

all the days that they are living on earth, and that they will also teach [this to] their children."
— Devarim 4:9-10

A. Conclusive proof for Moshe's prophecy

How do we know that the Revelation at Mount Sinai is the only conclusive proof that [Moshe's] prophecy was true? For it is written, "I am going to come to you in the thickness of the cloud, so that the people may hear when I speak with you, and they will also believe in you forever" (Shemos 19:9). The [verse] implies that, before this, they did not have firm, everlasting belief in him; their faith until then allowed for doubt and [second] thoughts.
— Rambam, Hilchos Yesodei HaTorah 8:1

There is a well-known question on the verse quoted by the Rambam (as he understood it): The verse seems to be saying that Israel fully believed in Moshe only after the Revelation; but did they not have this faith earlier, at the Splitting of the Sea — "They believed in Hashem and in Moshe His servant" (*Shemos* 14:31)?

In his elucidation of this verse (ibid. 19:9), the Ibn Ezra addresses this question:

The sages of India say that it is impossible for a human to survive after God speaks to him. There were Jews in Egypt who held the same belief and were thus doubtful of Moshe's prophecy. The verse, "They believed in Hashem and in Moshe His servant" (Shemos 14:31) does not challenge this fact, for there it says, "Israel saw," not "All of Israel," [but now they will all believe in you] .... "When I speak with you" and tell you the Ten Commandments, they will know that it is possible for humans to communicate with God and yet survive [the experience]. "And they will

believe in you" that you are a prophet because their doubt will be resolved. Indeed, the verse explicitly states: "Today we have seen that God can speak with a person and he will [still] survive" (Devarim 5:21). Another verse there states, "Who among flesh heard the word of the Living God speak from within the flames — as we have — and survived?" (ibid. v. 23). And there it is written [that Israel said to Moshe], "You draw near and listen to whatever Hashem, our God, says" (ibid. v. 24), and therefore, "they will also believe in you forever."
— Ibn Ezra, Shemos 19:9

According to the Ibn Ezra, then, before the Revelation not all the Jews were convinced of Moshe's prophecy, but the Revelation confirmed it for everyone.

B. The Revelation proved that Moshe reached the highest possible level of prophecy

But the Ramban disagrees with the Ibn Ezra's approach:

This is not correct, for the children of Avraham would never doubt prophecy, as they had always believed in it by tradition from their forefathers. Scripture already has stated: "The people believed [the signs], and they heard that Hashem had remembered the Children of Israel" (Shemos 4:31); "They believed in Hashem and in Moshe His servant" (ibid. 14:31). And though it does not say there, "and all the people [believed]" or "all Israel believed," neither does it say here "so that all the people may hear."

The correct [explanation of this verse] appears to me to be that [God] said [to Moshe,] "I am going to come to you in the thickness of the cloud: approach the thick cloud so that the people may hear when I speak, and they themselves will be prophets when I speak, without having to believe in it from others." [Likewise,] it is written, "When Hashem said to me, 'Assemble the people for Me and I will let them hear My words, so that they learn to fear Me all the days'" (Devarim 4:10).

"And they will also believe in you forever" — throughout the generations. If a prophet or dreamer arises in their midst who will contradict [your prophecy], they will immediately disprove him, for they will have seen and heard themselves that you reached the highest level of prophecy. This verse will be clear to them: "If there is a prophet among you, I, Hashem, reveal Myself to him [only] in a vision; in a dream I speak to him. Not so My servant, Moshe, who is trusted in My entire house — to him I speak mouth to mouth" (Bamidbar 12:6-7). That is why He said, "So that the people may hear when I speak with you," for they will hear My words from within the fire, and they will believe My word "and they will also believe in you forever." Similarly, when they said, "Today we have seen that God can speak with a person and he will [still] survive" (Devarim 5:21), they meant to say, "Now [Moshe's superior prophecy] has been confirmed to us by the sight of our own eyes, as God had wished." From now on, "You draw near" (ibid. 5:24), for we know that you have reached the uppermost level [of prophecy], "and listen to whatever Hashem, our God, says, and then you tell us whatever Hashem, our God, tells you; we will listen and do [it]" (ibid.), for your prophecy has been confirmed to be above that of all prophets [and cannot be overturned].

— Ramban, Shemos 19:9

We can summarize the Ramban's approach to the necessity of the Revelation as follows: None of the Jews ever had any doubts concerning the existence of prophecy, nor did they have any doubts regarding Moshe's prophecy. However, until the Revelation, there was no guarantee that Moshe's prophecy would forever be beyond the challenges of false prophets or "dreamers." But at the Revelation all the Jews saw for themselves that Moshe's level of prophecy was the highest level possible, so if anyone would ever claim that he was prophetically told by God to discard one of Moshe's teachings, he is obviously a fraud.

This approach, however, raises a question: How did the Revelation at Mount Sinai help them gain clarity that would last "forever"?

C. Prophets cannot deny Moshe's prophecy without undermining their own

Let us turn to the illuminating words of the Rambam in *Hilchos Yesodei HaTorah*:

> *Thus, [Israel], to whom [Moshe] was sent, are themselves the witnesses to the validity of Moshe's prophecy. He did not have to perform any signs for them [to prove himself], for he and they were like two witnesses who observed something together — neither witness has to prove the [honesty] of the other one. So too, after the Revelation at Mount Sinai, all of Israel [automatically became] witnesses to Moshe Rabbeinu — there was no need to do any signs for them....*
>
> *Consequently, when a prophet after Moshe Rabbeinu presents himself, we trust him not only because of the sign [he foretold] — we would not say: "If he does a sign, we will listen to whatever he says" — but because of Moshe's instruction in the Torah to listen to someone who presents a sign (see Devarim 18:15). Just as he instructed us to determine facts by [the testimony of] two witnesses — even though we don't really know whether they testified truthfully or lied — so too, there is a mitzvah to listen to a prophet [who predicted signs] — even though we do not know whether the signs were real or mere sorcery and magic.*
>
> *Therefore, if a prophet arose and did great signs and wonders, but then tried to deny the prophecy of Moshe Rabbeinu, we would not listen to him. We would also know clearly that those signs were done with magic and*

sorcery. Since Moshe's prophecy is not based on signs, we would not reject [Moshe's] signs merely because of the signs of the other. Rather, we saw [the prophecy] with our own eyes and heard it with our own ears exactly as he heard it. To what can this be compared? To witnesses who [attempted] telling a person who saw an event that it was not as he saw; he will not listen to them, for he knows with certainty that they are false witnesses. The Torah therefore said that [even] if the sign and wonder [predicted by the false prophet] came about, "You must not heed the words of that prophet" (ibid. 13:4), for he is [using] a sign or wonder to deny what you saw with your eyes. Since the only reason we believe in wonders is because of the instruction commanded to us by Moshe, how could we possibly accept signs that strive to deny the prophecy of Moshe, which we heard and saw for ourselves?

— Rambam, Hilchos Yesodei HaTorah 8:1

In short, since the only reason we would believe a prophet is because Moshe commanded us to do so, if a prophet would deny Moshe's prophecy, there would also be no basis for his prophecy! Even if his claim was based on a sign he predicted, we would still not accept him, for a sign that contradicts a witnessed event is — worthless.

D. The benefit of remembering the Revelation

All would agree, then, that the Jews' ability to see Moshe's prophecy and stature for themselves was a fundamental aspect of the Revelation. The Ramban alludes to this idea briefly in *Parshas Yisro* (cited in section B, above), and elaborates on it in *Parshas Va'eschanan*:

In my opinion, this verse ["However, be careful..." (Devarim 4:9)] is a negative commandment. [Moshe] warned them severely because after he told us to watch all the laws and decrees [ibid. v. 6], he repeated his warning to "beware and guard yourself very carefully" and remember the source of all these commandments; you should not forget the Revelation at Sinai and all the things that your eyes beheld: "the sounds," "the torches," "His Glory," "And His words you heard from within the fire." [And he told them to] inform "all the things that your eyes beheld" at that glorious event to "your children and grandchildren" forever. He then explained why [they should do so]: because Hashem made that Assembly in order for you to learn to fear Him forever and [so that] you teach [about it] to your children for all future generations. Therefore, do so and do not forget it.

Now, before mentioning the Commandments that were said there, He warned us with a negative commandment that we should never forget any detail of that event and He commanded with a positive commandment that we should inform all our descendants from generation to generation of all the sights and sounds that were there.

The benefit of this mitzvah is great, for if the words of the Torah would have come to us only through Moshe, even though his prophecy was confirmed through signs and wonders, [yet] if a prophet would ever arise at some later time and would command us in any matter to the contrary of the Torah, and provide us with a sign — then doubt would enter people's hearts. But because the Torah came to our ears directly from the Almighty, and our eyes saw [the giving of the Torah] without any intermediary, we can then disprove any dissenter and any doubter. No sign will help him and no wonder will save him from death at our hands, for we know his deceit.

Thus it is written, "And they will also believe in you forever" (ibid. 19:9), for when we repeat it for our children, they will know that the matter is undoubtedly the truth — it will be as though all the generations had seen it. For we do not testify lies to our children, nor do we bequeath nonsense and useless [information] to them. They will not doubt our testimony; on the contrary, they will believe with certitude that we all saw with our own eyes whatever we have recounted to them.

— Ramban, Devarim 4:9

E. Where the Rambam and the Ramban differ

Both the Rambam and the Ramban, then, agree that our witnessing the Revelation protects us from false prophets. But they differ on how this is accomplished. According to the Rambam, the only reason we believe prophets in the first place is because Moshe commanded us to follow them, and he also commanded us to ignore any prophet that preaches against Moshe's teachings, so if a prophet contradicts Moshe, he automatically loses his authority. But according to the Ramban we can tell that someone is a false prophet as soon as he gives an instruction that is against the Torah, because we heard the Torah ourselves along with Moshe and we know that we were not taught as this "prophet" claims. The Ramban's approach leaves out the idea that we only follow prophets because Moshe instructed us to believe them. One practical difference between these two approaches is how to understand a certain passage in the *Mechilta*, cited by the Ramban in *Parshas Yisro*:

I have seen [the following] in the Mechilta: "'So that the people may hear when I speak with you' — this teaches that the Holy One, Blessed is He, said to Moshe, 'I am going to call you from the top of the mountain, and you will come up,' as it is said, 'Hashem called Moshe [to the peak of the mountain and Moshe went up]' (Shemos 19:20). 'And they will also believe in you forever' — that is, '[they will believe] in you and also in the prophets who are destined to arise after you'" (Mechilta, Shemos 19:9). The words of the Mechilta incline toward the opinion of Rabbi Avraham [Ibn Ezra]

— Ramban, Shemos 19:9

The Ramban means that this *Mechilta* supports the Ibn Ezra's position that there was a time when Jews did not believe in prophecy. But now, because of the Revelation, they will believe "in the prophets who are destined to arise after you." By contrast, the way the Ramban understood the verse, it is not referring at all to future prophets but only to the permanence of Moshe's prophecy, as we discussed above.

There is, however, another way to understand the *Mechilta.* To see how, let us look again at the Rambam's words: "When a prophet after Moshe Rabbeinu presents himself, we trust him not only because of the sign ... but because of Moshe's instruction ... to listen to someone who presents a sign." Consequently, belief in future prophets is dependent on the validity of Moshe's prophecy. Whenever a prophet negates even one letter of Moshe's instructions, he completely discredits himself. Since the trustworthiness of future prophets is only possible because it is included in Moshe's command, it therefore makes sense that the *Mechilta* would find an allusion to future prophets in the verse, "And they will also believe in you forever." This *Mechilta,* therefore, does not prove the Ibn Ezra's position that Jews did not originally believe in prophecy; perhaps they always did, but the *Mechilta* was discussing the institution of prophecy in the future.

F. "Fear of Hashem is pure; it endures forever"

We began this chapter with a question from the verse, "They believed in Hashem and in Moshe His servant" (*Shemos* 14:31), which seems to contradict the Rambam's opinion that the Jews only came to believe in Moshe with the experience of the Revelation. We now see that, according to the Rambam, the Jews always believed in prophecy and in the legitimacy of Moshe; however, their faith was not firm enough to last forever. "The [verse] implies that prior to this, they did not have firm, everlasting belief in him; their faith until then allowed for doubt and [second] thoughts" (*Hilchos Yesodei HaTorah* 8:1). Their faith in prophecy, maintained the Rambam, was too frail to last forever. God therefore gave them the Revelation at Sinai and infused them with fear, as is written, "God has come ... in order that reverence for Him be impressed upon you, so that you do not sin" (*Shemos* 20:17). Once fear of God was etched on their faces, their memories of that event would remain firm, as is written, "The fear of Hashem is pure; it endures forever" (*Tehillim* 19:10).

Accordingly, the Rambam's position can be summarized with the eloquent words of the *Kuzari*:

> *Even the sages of the Children of Israel challenged [Moshe] because they did not fully believe him that God spoke to man until they heard the Ten Commandments from [God]. His own nation treated him this way, not because of ignorance but because of their wisdom. They wanted to be certain that he was not deceiving them with magic, astrological arts, or similar fraud that — like counterfeit coins — would not stand up to close examination. Not so Divine matters that are like pure gold: the closer they are examined the more value they are seen to possess.*
> *— Kuzari, Part I, 49*

G. The power of the Revelation continues to our day

The lessons of the Revelation have lasted throughout the ages because it was so momentous. But it is most important that we realize that we are constantly re-experiencing it. Just as the Giving of the Torah was not a one-time event but a continuous one — as the blessings for Torah study convey: "He Who teaches the Torah .... He Who gives the Torah" — so too, God's Revelation continues. We thus find that when our Sages engaged themselves in Torah study, a Heavenly fire would descend upon them, just as it did at Sinai (see *Chagigah* 15 and *Koheles Rabbah* 7).

The practical application for us is that if we as individuals wish to experience the Revelation, then we — like our ancestors — must prepare ourselves and sanctify ourselves. We will then merit drawing the essentials of faith from that deep wellspring of faith. How do we do this? By studying the Torah. Conversely, when our Torah study falters, our faith also falters, Heaven forbid. Let us reinforce our devotion to Torah study and, with it, our faith will be reinforced — to last forever.

CHAPTER THIRTEEN

The Accuracy of Our Tradition

A. Two Chains of Tradition

We have two sources for our faith in the Unity of God. The first is a tradition from our forefathers, beginning with Avraham Avinu, who was the chief of all believers.

Avraham himself came to believe in God by three routes: Contemplation, study, and prophecy, as we shall see. Avraham possessed a pure mind and superb character traits. With these, he contemplated the origins of the world and he gained great wisdom and insight, until it became absolutely clear to him that there must be only one, true Creator. He wrote books and gave many lectures on the topic. The arguments he presented against all the popular pagan notions of his day were clear and irrefutable. He won all debates. Thus, hundreds and thousands of people — known as "Avraham's household" — became his followers. (See above, Chapter Four.)

Avraham also studied under Shem, who was one of the few people who had an unbroken tradition from Adam HaRishon that God is One and that He created the world.

Finally, God revealed Himself to him by prophecy and spoke to him many times. For example, after Avraham showed he was willing to give up his life (in Ur Kasdim) for his belief in God's Unity, God appeared to him and told him, "Go away from your land" (*Bereishis* 12:1). This was the culmination of his search for God. Our Sages described Avraham's quest with a parable:

> *There was once a man who traveled from place to place. [Once,] he saw a castle that was all lit up. He said to himself, "Can it be that this castle has no owner?" [Just then] the owner of the castle peeked out, and told him, "I am the owner of the castle." So too, Avraham Avinu had been saying, "Can it be that this world has no Owner?" [So] the Holy One "peeked out" at him and told him, "I am the Master of the world."*
>
> — *Bereishis Rabbah 39:1*

Can there be a clearer proof for God's existence than when He appears to someone in a prophetic vision?

Avraham then conveyed his insights, tradition, and experiences to his son Yitzchak, who passed them on to his son Yaakov and so on.

B. For all to see

The second source of our faith began at Mount Sinai. When the Holy One chose us to be His "treasured nation" (see *Shemos* 19:5) who would sanctify His Name in the world, He wished to establish us on a foundation of everlasting faith. This would be accomplished by showing Himself to the whole nation. God therefore descended "on Mount Sinai in the sight of all the people" (ibid. v. 11) and was not satisfied with giving the Torah and the mitzvos through Moshe alone. All would see His Glory "face to face" (*Devarim* 5:4), and all would hear His voice declare, "I am Hashem, your God.... You shall not have any other gods before Me" (*Shemos* 20:2-3). Our Sages therefore emphasized the fact that "We heard 'I am,' and 'You shall not,' from the mouth of the Almighty" (*Horayos* 8a); meaning, we heard the foundation of our faith in God's Unity directly from God Himself.

C. The best setting at the best time

Thus God appeared "in the sight of all the people," which included 600,000 adult men between the ages of 20 and 60 plus many more women and children, and men over the age of 60. God did not appear to them immediately after freeing them from their intense servitude, when their bodies and spirits were still in pain from backbreaking labor and the torment of imminent annihilation. Instead, He waited until they were all in a tranquil frame of mind and were well rested from the horrors they had suffered in Egypt. During the long period of the Plagues in Egypt, when the Egyptians were too busy with their own problems, the Jewish people's wounds had time to heal. And the special provisions given to them in the desert — the Well, the Manna, and Clouds of Glory — further cured all their defects, invigorated them, and gave them shelter. By the time they experienced the Revelation, their minds were open to attain wisdom and prophecy, and they were settled enough to perceive and to understand what they would be shown.

They were also spiritually ready for the Revelation. First, the master of all prophets, Moshe, prepared them; second, they sanctified themselves; and, third, the Holy One purified the world's air of the pollution of false notions and twisted thinking with the "thunder and lightning." The thunder and lightning was so intense and so terrifying that the nations of the world came to ask Bilam whether God was planning on drowning the world again!

God made the Revelation an overwhelming experience, with the mountain "blazing with fire to the very heart of the heavens" (*Devarim* 4:11) and with God's voice "speaking from within the fire" (ibid. v. 33) and from all directions (see *Shemos Rabbah* 5:9).

No creature in the world can make sounds that loud and for that long; it was "a great voice that did not cease" (*Devarim* 5:19), for the "voice of Hashem [comes] in power" (*Tehillim* 29:4).

When the Jews heard God's voice and they saw His majesty, their souls slipped out of them — "for no person can see Me and live" (*Shemos* 33:20) — until God brought them back to life. Even then, they were so frightened that they retreated twelve *mil* and needed the angels to help them return (see *Shabbos* 88b and *Rashi* to *Shemos* 20:15).

Indeed, they saw that it is "Hashem Who is God; there is none other besides Him" (*Devarim* 4:35).

D. A generation with clarity

Israel now realized that they were created anew as a nation of believers. They sensed the faith in God and in his servant Moshe becoming firmly etched on their hearts. Still, it was a terrifying experience, so after hearing the first two Commandments directly from God, they asked Moshe, "You speak with us, and let us hear, but let God not speak with us, so that we do not die" (*Shemos* 20:16). But this does not mean that they did not hear the rest of God's Utterances, as the Ramban explains:

> *All of Israel certainly heard the entire Ten Commandments from God, as the plain reading of the verse implies ["God spoke all these words ...." (Shemos 20:1)]. However, they heard and understood the first two Commandments as Moshe understood them, which is why [they are in the first person]; but from then on, they could hear the sound of the Utterance but were unable to comprehend it, and so it was necessary for Moshe to translate each Commandment until they understood it.*
>
> — *Ramban, Shemos 20:1*

Then, after hearing each Commandment, they affirmed whatever they heard: They said "Yes, [we will]" to all the positive instructions and "No, [we will not]" to all the things they were instructed to refrain from.

That entire generation, then, reached the peak of human insight and were all complete believers. They were firmly attached to the Source of Life. How lofty their level must have been if they could declare: "Hashem, our God, has indeed shown us His glory and His greatness, and we have heard His voice from within the fire. Today we have seen that God can speak with a person and he will still live" (*Devarim* 5:21)!

E. Future generations

But theirs was not the only generation to experience the Revelation; the souls of all future generations of Jews were there, and they all breathed deeply from that air of faith and prophecy. Thus it is written, "And not with you alone am I forming this covenant and this oath, but with those who are standing here with us today, before Hashem, our God, and with those who are not here with us today" (*Devarim* 29:13-14). In fact, our Sages teach that anyone who doubts the principles of faith and veers from the path that was laid out at Sinai "is not a descendant of the people who stood there!" (*Rambam, Iggeres Teiman*). That is, the Revelation at Sinai changed the descendants of Avraham, Yitzchak, and Yaakov to the point that faith has become part of their inborn nature. It brought out the core of their souls and restored the original purity of man's heart: "God has made man straight, but they sought many [sinful] schemes" (*Koheles* 7:29). Man was created full of faith and good, but the sinners dimmed the light of their souls and corrupted themselves.

F. Not a one-time event

Don't, however, make the mistake of thinking that the Revelation was a one-time event. The Revelation continues to this day because it has been incorporated into the Torah which is a living entity. When we study the Torah, and when we keep its commandments, we once again make ourselves "straight" and we delight in the glow of faith, for "The orders of Hashem are upright; they gladden the heart" (*Tehillim* 19:9), and "Light is sown for the righteous; and for the upright of heart, gladness" (ibid. 97:11). The "light" that is sown for the righteous is the light of Hashem, the light of faith that shone forth at the Giving of the Torah.

G. All the generations are connected

In a sense, we all saw and heard the Giving of the Torah along with our ancestors, for all the generation since then are part of one chain. Each generation of Jews feels connected to the previous one. We feel — like the first generation of "children" felt — that we witnessed the Revelation ourselves. We are confident with our tradition and we know that our parents are telling us the truth. Parents "do not testify lies" to their children, as the Ramban (*Shemos* 4:9) put it. Look at the immense efforts that observant Jewish parents invest in passing on this tradition to their children. Even those who, for whatever reason, are estranged from the Torah do not willingly pass on misinformation. At most they are ignorant. Thus, it is still unthinkable that any Jewish parent would intentionally lie to their children about our past. Besides, the Torah itself is very convincing evidence — "The testimony of Hashem is trustworthy" (*Tehillim* 19:8). "Those who have tasted it," says the Shabbos Siddur, "merit life," and anyone who has seriously studied Torah knows that it is true.

H. One of the many chains of tradition

We possess an unbroken chain of tradition from the Exodus and the Revelation until our generation. Here we have included a list of forty generations as recorded in the Rambam:

> *From Rav Ashi [going back] to Moshe Rabbeinu there are forty generations: (1) Rav Ashi [received] from Rava; (2) Rava from Rabbah; (3) Rabbah from Rav Huna; (4) Rav Huna from R' Yochanan, Rav, and Shmuel; (5) R' Yochanan, Rav, and Shmuel from Rabbeinu HaKadosh; (6) Rabbeinu HaKadosh from his father, Rabi Shimon [III]; (7) Rabi Shimon [III] from his father, Rabban*

Gamliel [II]; (8) Rabban Gamliel [II] from his father, Rabi Shimon [II]; (9) Rabi Shimon [II] from his father, Rabban Gamliel [the Elder]; (10) Rabban Gamliel the Elder from his father, Rabi Shimon [I]; (11) Rabi Shimon [I] from his father, Hillel and from Shamai; (12) Hillel and Shamai from Shmaya and Avtalion; (13) Shmaya and Avtalion from Yehudah and Shimon; (14) Yehudah and Shimon from Yehoshua ben Perachia and Nitai HaArbeili; (15) Yehoshua and Nitai from Yose ben Yoezer and Yosef ben Yochanan; (16) Yose ben Yoezer and Yosef ben Yochanan from Antigonos; (17) Antigonos from Shimon HaTzaddik; (18) Shimon HaTzaddik from Ezra; (19) Ezra from Baruch; (20) Baruch from Yirmiyah; (21) Yirmiyah from Tzefania; (22) Tzefania from Chavakkuk; (23) Chavakkuk from Nachum; (24) Nachum from Yoel; (25) Yoel from Michah; (26) Michah from Yeshayah; (27) Yeshayah from Amos; (28) Amos from Hoshea; (29) Hoshea from Zechariah; (30) Zechariah from Yehoyada; (31) Yehoyada from Elisha; (32) Elisha from Eliyahu; (33) Eliyahu from Achiyah; (34) Achiyah from David; (35) David from Shmuel; (36) Shmuel from Eli; (37) Eli from Pinchas; (38) Pinchas from Yehoshua; (39) Yehoshua from Moshe Rabbeinu; (40) Moshe Rabbeinu from the Almighty. Thus they all [have a tradition] from Hashem, the God of Israel!

All of the sages mentioned here were the greatest people of their [respective] generations. Some of them were Roshei Yeshivah (Heads of Academies), others were Exilarchs, while still others were members of the Great Sanhedrin. [Add to] them the thousands, if not tens of thousands, [of students] who heard [Torah] from them and with them.

— Rambam, Introduction to Yad HaChazakah

The Rambam's list concludes with Rav Ashi. He and Ravina were the last of the Sages of the Talmud. After the Sages of the Talmud, the chain of tradition continued with the Rabbanan Savorai, to the Geonim, to the Rishonim, and then to the Acharonim. Thus the halachic authorities of our generation are the newest links in this uninterrupted chain of tradition. Many of the Sages in this chain also wrote books which we still study and apply to our lives. What other nation can claim such an ironclad tradition through thousands of years of history, all the way back to Sinai?

I. Outside verification

Many of our accounts of events that happened in antiquity are also recorded in world history and have been verified by archeological findings. The scholars of the world (including non-religious ones) know all this, and the only reason they don't embrace observance is because they approach whatever they study as "professionals," not as seekers of truth.

J. The age of the world

We also have a clear count of all the years since creation, which we use to number the years of our calendar. Indeed, we can trace all the generations since Adam HaRishon, for our ancestors made sure to maintain their lineage. Even when they were in Egypt, they knew how they descended from Avraham, Yitzchak, and Yaakov and how the forefathers descended from Adam, Shem, and Ever. (See above, Chapter Two, sections A, D, and E.)

Again, our tradition is from people who saw these events themselves, from people who investigated, clarified, and ascertained the truth. And we will continue this tradition to the next generation. We can therefore easily refute anybody who dares to deny our tradition, as the Rambam so forcefully put it: "To what can this be compared? To witnesses who [attempted] telling a person who saw an event that it was not as he saw; he will not listen to them, for he knows with certainty that they are false witnesses" (*Rambam, Hilchos Yesodei HaTorah* 8:1).

K. Imitations

Our religion is very different from all other religions. All other religions are based on the say-so of their founder, their "prophet." Typically, the founder claims that he received a divine message instructing him to "reveal" himself and preach a new religion. These "revelations" always occurred, of course, when the founder was alone.

In contrast, our religion is based on a revelation witnessed by an entire nation. Of this it is written, "I did not speak in secrecy at first" (*Yeshayah* 48:16).

To simple-minded people the world's religions may appear genuine, but the truth is, they are shams. Compared to Judaism, they are like a scarecrow's resemblance to a human: an animal may think a scarecrow is a real person, but a human will never be fooled by it (the Rambam, in *Iggeres Teiman* gives a similar parable).

Christianity and Islam, in particular, are simply cheap imitations of Judaism. (For a clear unmasking of their deceit, see the Rambam's *Iggeres Teiman.*) In the first essay of the *Kuzari*, both the Christian scholar and the Islamic one concede to the king of the Kuzars that their religions rely on the teachings of Moshe Rabbeinu. After hearing this, the Kuzar says, "I see, then, that the only ones I should ask [about the possibility of communicating with God] are the Jews, for they are the remnant of the Children of Israel. I see that they are themselves the proof that God has a Torah on earth" (*Kuzari*, first essay).

CHAPTER FOURTEEN

"We Will Do and We Will Listen"

A. Commitment vs. performance

When Israel [declared] "We will do" (Shemos 24:7) before "We will listen," a [Heavenly] voice went out and said to them, "[This is the secret] used by the ministering angels, as is written, 'Bless Hashem, O His angels; the strong warriors who do His bidding, to listen to the voice of His word' (Tehillim 103:20) — first [they] 'do' and then [they] 'listen.' Who revealed this secret to My Children?"
— Shabbos 88a

Why is this such as secret, and how, indeed can you do something before you listen to the instructions? We can ask a similar question on the Mishnah in *Pirkei Avos*: "Anyone whose good deeds exceed his wisdom, his wisdom will endure; but anyone whose wisdom exceeds his good deeds, his wisdom will not endure" (*Avos* 3:12). "How is it possible," asks Rabbeinu Yonah, "for someone's deeds to be more than his wisdom? If he does not know the Torah and the mitzvos, how can he keep them?" He answers:

> *This Mishnah is giving sound advice to someone who does not know [that much], telling him how to preserve his soul. He should accept upon himself to obey the Sages, without deviating right or left from whatever they tell him, whenever he [eventually] learns those laws. [And he should accept upon himself] to act in accord with the Torah which they will instruct him and the laws they will tell him. As soon as he willingly and wholeheartedly accepts this upon himself, he will immediately receive reward as though he had accepted all the [individual] mitzvos upon himself.*
>
> *This is what the phrase, "Anyone whose good deeds exceed his wisdom" means. For even someone who does not know and does not do [the mitzvos] can nevertheless be considered as one who did do them since — as a result of his pledge — he already receives the reward of someone who has done them.*
>
> *This [explanation] is the explicit reading of Avos D'Rabi Nosson: "Anyone whose good deeds exceed his wisdom, his wisdom will endure, as is written, 'We will do and we will listen.'" Israel placed doing before hearing when they should have said, "We will listen and we will do," because before you can do anything you have to know what you are expected to do. What Israel were saying, however, was that they committed themselves from the outset to do whatever [God] will eventually command them and*

they will listen; so they immediately received reward as though they had actually performed [the commandments].
— *Rabbeinu Yonah, Avos 3:12*

From this commentary, we can see why "doing before hearing" is such a special "secret," for it is a way to receive immense reward before actually performing the mitzvos.

B. How do we know that commitment garners the reward of actually doing the mitzvos?

That "doing before hearing" means "making a commitment" to do whatever we will be taught, needs no further proof; there is no other way to "do" something before you know what you will be asked to do. But how did Rabbeinu Yonah know that as soon as they committed to keeping the Torah "they immediately received reward as though they had actually performed them"? We might be tempted to answer that he understood this from the Gemara: "When Israel [declared] 'We will do' (*Shemos* 24:7) before 'We will listen,' 600,000 angels came and tied two crowns to the head of each and every Jew, one for 'we will do' and one for 'we will listen'" (*Shabbos* 88a). However, one could argue that those "crowns" were not reward for doing the mitzvos but only for the single act of making the commitment.

Perhaps Rabbeinu Yonah derived it from the fact that the Gemara compared the Jews' commitment to the angels "secret," of whom the verse says that they "do His bidding, to listen to the voice of His word" (*Tehillim* 103:20). There it is clear that although they were only "prepared to do" God's will (*Rashi* ad loc.) the verse refers to them as though they actually do God's will (they "do His bidding"). Thus willingness to do is tantamount to doing, for which, of course, there is reward.

C. God's omniscience

Until now we have been focusing on the Exodus as the source of faith. But there is another important principle that emerged from the Exodus: The obligation to accept upon ourselves the yoke of Heaven. From then on we were to view ourselves as God's servants. This idea is expressed in the following verse: "For [the Children of Israel] are My servants, whom I took out of the land of Egypt. They must not be sold in the same way as slaves" (*Vayikra* 25:42). Rashi there explains that we may not sell fellow Jews as slaves because God says, "My [ownership] document precedes [yours]" so that you all belong to Me — and a slave cannot sell another slave.

The Torah prohibits taking interest on loans (*ribbis*). Why? Because "I am Hashem, your God, Who took you out of the land of Egypt" (ibid. v. 38). How does this explain why we are not allowed to charge interest? Rashi offers two answers:

> *"[I am Hashem, your God,] Who took you out [of the land of Egypt] and distinguished between those who were firstborn and those who were not firstborn, I also know [the true facts of this matter] and I will exact punishment from one who lends money to a Jew while claiming that it belongs to a non-Jew."*
>
> *Another explanation is : "[I am Hashem, your God,] Who took you out of the land of Egypt" on condition that you take upon yourselves [to fulfill] My commands even when they are hard for you."*
>
> *— Rashi, Vayikra 25:38*

These two explanations reflect the two main principles that we were to take from the Exodus. The first is faith in God and in His knowledge, and the second is that we accepted the yoke of God upon ourselves, as we will discuss in section D.

The fact that God could tell which of the Egyptians were firstborn — even when people thought they were not — is a primary example of God's knowledge of this world's affairs. This is why this plague is attributed directly to God: "I will pass through the land of Egypt on that night — I, and not an angel" (*Pesach Haggadah,* from *Shemos* 12:12), and why "I am going to kill your firstborn son" (ibid. 4:23) was the very first, and most terrifying, warning relayed to Pharaoh. Indeed, of all of God's revelations in Egypt, this was the greatest show of God's omniscience: "The Egyptian women were unfaithful to their husbands and bore children from young, unmarried men; and thus [the Egyptian women] had many firstborn sons — sometimes there were five to one woman, each being the firstborn to his [true] father" (*Rashi, Shemos* 12:30), yet God was able to "distinguish in Egypt between a 'drop' [that would be] a firstborn and one not of a firstborn" (*Rashi, Bamidbar* 15:41). The people obviously could not tell them apart, but God could.

God thus showed at the Plague of the Firstborn that He sees everything, even the most private and lowly actions. This contradicted the heretics who thought that "Hashem has forsaken the land" (*Yechezkel* 8:12), or that it is beneath God's dignity to look at our inferior world. My teacher, Rabbi Eliyahu Lopian *zt"l*, explained that this is why the nations believe that "High above all nations is Hashem" (*Tehillim* 113:4), that He has removed His gaze from this world and now only "above the heavens is His glory." But we respond, "Who is like Hashem, our God" (ibid. v. 5). Who shows providence more than our God. Who else does so many wonders and miracles for us? For although He "is enthroned on high, yet [He] deigns to look upon the heavens and the earth" (ibid. v. 6) — heaven and earth are equal before Him!

D. Becoming God's servants

Rashi's second comment highlights the principle that the Exodus was cause for us to accept God's absolute sovereignty. God took us out of Egypt "on condition that you take upon yourselves [to fulfill] My commands even when they are hard for you." Similarly, the first of the Ten Commandments, "I am Hashem, your God, Who took you out of the land of Egypt, out of the house of slavery" (*Shemos* 20:2), includes both the concept of belief in God and of accepting His sovereignty. According to most commentators, this verse is a commandment to believe in God's power, but it also alludes to the fact that "It was worthwhile taking you out of Egypt so that you will subject yourselves to Me" (*Rashi, Shemos* 20:2) and accept God's sovereignty.

The Ramban on this verse shows how the two concepts intersect:

> *"I am Hashem, your God" — this Utterance is a positive commandment. He said, "I am Hashem," to teach and command them that they should know and believe that Hashem exists and that He is God to them. That is, that there is an Eternal Being through Whom everything has come into existence by His will and power; He is God to them, and they are obligated to worship Him. He [then] said, "Who took you out of the land of Egypt," because the fact that He took them out from there demonstrates [His] existence and will, for it was with His knowledge and providence that [they] came out from there. It also showed that [the world was a] new creation, for [if] it is assumed that the universe is eternal, [it would follow that] nothing would ever change from its nature. And it also showed God's infinite power; and His infinite power demonstrates His Unity, as He said, "So that you will realize that there are none like Me in the whole world" (Shemos 9:14). For the same reason [the verse includes] "Who took you out," since they are the ones who know and witnessed all these things.*
>
> *The meaning of "out of the house of slavery" is that they stayed in Egypt in a house of bondage as captives of Pharaoh. He said this to them [so that they will understand] that they are obligated [to accept] this great, glorious and fearful Name as their God — that is to serve Him — because he redeemed them from the servitude of Egypt. It is similar in meaning [to the verse], "They are My servants whom I took out of the land of Egypt" (Vayikra 25:55)....*
>
> *This commandment, in the words of our Rabbis, is called "accepting the sovereignty of Heaven" (see Berachos 13a).... Thus the [Sages] said in the Mechilta: "'You shall have no other gods before Me.' Why is this said? Because it says, 'I am Hashem, your God.' [This can be*

understood with] a parable: A king invaded a country, and his [new subjects, the] servants, said to him, 'Issue decrees to us.' He said to them, 'No! When you accept my sovereignty, I will issue decrees to you. For if you are not willing to accept my sovereignty, how [can I trust that you will] carry out my decrees?' Similarly, God said to Israel: 'I am Hashem, your God.... You shall not have [any other gods].' Am I the One Whose sovereignty you accepted in Egypt?' 'Yes,' they replied. 'Well, then, just as you have accepted My sovereignty upon yourselves, accept My decrees.' That is, now that you have admitted and accepted upon yourselves that I am Hashem and I am your God since [the time you were] in Egypt, then you [must] accept all of My commandments."

— *Ramban, Shemos 20:2*

The Ramban has made it very clear to us that recalling the Exodus is not only a matter of recognition or belief but a mitzvah that demands duty and service, of "accepting the sovereignty of Heaven." By extension, we may infer that whenever the Torah alludes to the Exodus as a source of belief in God, it is really referring to the consequence of that belief, which is our obligation to accept God's sovereignty. Thus the title the Rambam gives for the first Commandment is "Accepting the Sovereignty of Heaven."

E. Mitzvos with both messages

Our Sages ordained that we say the "portion of *tzitzis*" (*Bamidbar* 15:37-41) as part of *Krias Shema.* The main reason we say this portion every day is to fulfill the mitzvah of recalling the Exodus. But why should we fulfill this mitzvah specifically together with the *Shema,* which is the acceptance of God's sovereignty? We now understand that, at its root, recalling the Exodus is also an expression of accepting God's sovereignty.

Tefillin is another example of a mitzvah that on one level is a reminder of the Exodus (see *Shemos* 13) but on another level is an act of allegiance to God. Thus the declaration of intent that is customarily recited before donning *tefillin* refers specifically to committing ourselves to serve God: "He has commanded us to put [*tefillin*] upon the arm ... opposite the heart to thereby subjugate the desires and thoughts of our heart to His service, may His Name be blessed; and upon the head near the brain, together with my other senses and potentials, so that they may all be subjugated to His service, may His Name be blessed." Rabbeinu Yonah (*Berachos* 14b, s.v. *Harotzeh*) likewise demonstrates how *tefillin* encourages accepting God's sovereignty.

F. Complete surrender to God's will

The fact that the Jews said "we will do" before "we will listen" now takes on new depth. For saying "we will do" first was not merely an act of special piety, beyond what was expected of them, but a precondition for receiving the Torah. They were duty-bound to make this commitment because of the servitude to God demanded by the Exodus. When it comes to servitude to God — to Whom everything belongs — there is no allowance for thinking like ordinary servants, "Let me first hear what the job entails" or "Will I be able to follow the instructions?" Rather, they completely subjugated themselves to God's will and accepted upon themselves to "do" His will no matter what they would be asked to do. They will listen to know what their assignment is and how they are to execute it. This commitment is what set us aside from all the nations, for when God attempted to give the Torah to the nations of the world, they asked, "What is written in it?" (*Yalkut Shimoni* §286). That is, they wanted to "listen" before they were willing to commit to "doing" anything for God. All they were really willing to do was what fit with their hearts' desires. That attitude is not considered accepting the yoke of Heaven.

A heretic once said to Rava, "Reckless nation! You put your mouths before your ears. You are still rash! You should have first listened to see if you could [keep it]; if yes, you would have accepted it, but if not, not" (*Shabbos* 88a). It is significant that it was a heretic who said this to Rava, for the real drive behind heresy is a desire to follow one's own mind and heart, as our

Sages expounded, "'Do not follow your hearts' (*Bamidbar* 15:39) — this refers to heresy" (*Berachos* 12b). This also explains why our Sages said that "Adam HaRishon was a heretic" (*Sanhedrin* 38b), for he, too, followed his heart instead of God's instruction.

G. The Tree of Life — doing before hearing

Adam's sin, on a deeper level, was that he did not say to himself "I will do" regardless of what I understand; he placed "I will listen" before "I will do." This way of looking at Adam's sin is based on the explanation of Adam's sin that I heard from Rabbi Eliyahu Dessler *zt"l*, in the name of R' Chaim of Volozhin. He explained that Adam faced a choice about choices; his decision would determine the nature of his free will. Stretched out before him were two paths to serving God. The first was called "the Tree of Life." Walking down that path would lead to complete self-effacement; he would have no opinion or inclination about his actions and he would have no sense of good and bad; he would trust and rely on God alone. He would nullify himself. The second path was "the Tree of Knowledge." On this path he would know and sense the difference between "good" and "bad." Adam chose the second path.

Why did he choose the path of the Tree of Knowledge? We can answer this question with a parable: A king once gave his servant permission to eat any of the dishes prepared in the palace. "But," he warned him, "do not eat this one." While the king was away, the king's maidservant told her husband, the king's servant, to taste the forbidden food so she would know how to prepare and serve this dish to the king with the right amount of flavorings and spices. While there was logic in the maidservant's action — it is important to know how to prepare the food — yet it violated the king's instruction. Similarly, Adam wanted to know "how to prepare the King's 'food,'" how to determine on his own what God wants from this world. Nevertheless, it was a sin to ignore God's explicit command.

We see, then, that the "Tree of Life" represents "doing before hearing," and the "Tree of Knowledge" represents the attitude of "let's hear before we do." Consequently, when Adam chose the path of the Tree of Knowledge, he became a "heretic" who preferred his own judgment over God's.

H. The Jews' commitment restored their Tree of Life

When Adam and Chavah committed the sin of the Tree of Knowledge, defilement from the snake entered them and death was decreed upon them. But this defilement ceased at the Revelation at Sinai (see *Shabbos* 146a), and they were freed from death and from the yoke of the nations. Perhaps they gained this freedom in the merit of their commitment of "We will do and we will listen." For this attitude stems from the "Tree of Life," and by making this commitment they corrected the sin of the Tree of Knowledge. They erased all calculations of personal gain and they nullified their will in an act of love of God. This gave them life because once they negated themselves they became attached to God, the Root of all life. As our Sages said in *Pirkei Avos*, "If someone takes upon himself the yoke of Torah, then the yoke of government and the yoke of worldly responsibilities are removed from him" (*Avos* 3:6). It all depends on one act of commitment.

By combining the idea that accepting God's will is the way we accept His sovereignty with an understanding of what is the purpose of the mitzvos, we can see even clearer why just making the commitment to do mitzvos can generate reward as though they were done. The Ramban at the end of *Parshas Bo* explains the purpose of the mitzvos:

> *The purpose of all the mitzvos is that we should believe in our God and acknowledge that He created us. [Indeed,] this is the purpose of the creation. For we have no other reason for the original creation. And the Almighty has no interest in the lower creatures except so that man should know and acknowledge to his God that He created him. Thus, the purpose for raising our voices in prayer, the purpose for synagogues, and the advantage of public prayer is*

so that people will have a place to gather to acknowledge to the Almighty that He created them and brought them forth. They will publicize this, and they will declare before Him: "We are your creatures!"
— *Ramban, Shemos 13:16*

When someone does a mitzvah he thereby acknowledges and demonstrates that God is the Master and he is the servant. Thus, each mitzvah is comprised of two elements: the act of the mitzvah and the submission to God that it expresses. And the reward each person receives for doing a mitzvah is based primarily on the faith and the acceptance of God's rule that it contained. This explains why if "someone planned on doing a mitzvah and was forced to forego doing it, Scripture nevertheless considers it done" (*Kiddushin* 40a), for as soon as the person planned on doing the mitzvah, he already submitted to God and acknowledged His sovereignty to the best of his abilities. And this also explains why our Sages said that we should "Be as scrupulous in performing a 'minor' mitzvah as a 'major' one" (*Avos* 2:1), "for all [mitzvos] are extremely precious and beloved, for through them a person consistently demonstrates his acknowledgement to his God" (*Ramban* ibid.).

I. Angels are messengers

Complete surrender to God's will is the hallmark of angels. The Hebrew word for "angel" is *malach,* which means "a messenger," because an angel is a creature whose essence is his mission. An angel is nothing but His Creator's messenger. This is why the name of an angel always refers to his mission — and if his mission is changed then his name is also changed — for a name describes the essence of an item. According to the Rambam, when God "speaks" to a prophet it is through an angel (except for the prophecy of Moshe Rabbeinu, which was "face to face"), yet it is still God speaking to the prophet because the angel is completely nullified to God's will and is not a barrier between God and the prophet. (Similarly, prophets are called *malachim* because they act as God's messengers to the people. Moshe, in particular, was called a *malach* [*Bamidbar* 20:16], for he was completely subservient to God and "the Divine Presence spoke from within his throat" [see *Mishnah Berurah* 428:6:18].) Thus when the Jews said, "We will do and we will listen," they were indeed acting like angels.

J. Preparing the pesach sacrifice

Earlier, we quoted Rabbeinu Yonah, who said, "This Mishnah is giving sound advice to someone who does not know [that much], telling him how to preserve his soul. He should accept upon himself to obey the Sages...." God Himself gave this "advice" to the Jews in Egypt. He instructed that each household should take a lamb and leave it "in your care until the fourteenth day of this month" (*Shemos* 12:6). Rashi explains:

> *Why did He order that it should be taken [from the flock] four days before its slaughter, something which He did not command [to be done] to the pesach sacrifice in succeeding generations? Rabbi Masia ben Charash said: [On the one hand, the verse] says, "And I passed by you and saw you, and behold, your time was the time of love" (Yechezkel 16:8) — the time has come [to fulfill] the oath which I had sworn to Avraham to redeem his children. [But on the other hand,] they had no mitzvos to engage in to [merit] being redeemed, as it says, "you were naked and bare" (ibid. v. 7). He therefore gave them two commands: the blood of the pesach sacrifice and the blood of circumcision.*
>
> *— Rashi, Shemos 12:6*

God told them to prepare for the pesach sacrifice because they had been "naked" of mitzvos. Thus, preparing for a mitzvah is considered doing the mitzvah, for otherwise how would setting aside the lambs give them the merit they were missing? Furthermore, the Torah tells us that they "went and did just as Hashem had commanded" (*Shemos* 12:28). "But did they really do this [at once] — was this not said at the beginning of the month [but they carried out the command only on the tenth and on the fourteenth]? But [the explanation is]: As soon as they had taken [these duties] upon themselves, Scripture considers it as though they had already performed them" (*Rashi*). By accepting upon themselves to do God's will, and by setting aside the lambs, they were no longer "naked of the mitzvos" and they had gained enough merit to be saved.

K. Why two crowns?

In section B we quoted the Sages about the two "crowns" the Jews received when they declared "we will do" before "we will listen," and in section F we learned that placing "we will do" before "we will listen" was a precondition for receiving the Torah. Accordingly, had they said "we will listen" first, they would not have received even one crown, which means that what really mattered was the fact that they said "we will do" first. But then why did they receive two crowns — it would seem that they only did one special act? The answer is that while it is true that receiving the Torah depended on their placing "we will do" first, yet once they did place it first, they deserved reward for both parts of their declaration. For there is also something special about saying "we will listen." In general, "we will listen" means that they committed themselves to focus only on God's words in the Torah, and not to be distracted by any wisdom that come from human hearts and minds. Their pledge to listen to God can be divided into four components. The first is: We are only interested in what God wants of us, not what we want. Second: We must delve into the Torah constantly. This point is derived from a combination of verses. Scripture calls studying the Torah vigorously "walking" ("If you walk in My statutes" [*Vayikra* 26:3] — "If you will toil [in the study of] Torah." [*Rashi*]), and refraining from learning is "not listening" ("But if you do not listen to Me" [ibid. v. 14] — "to toil in Torah" [*Rashi*]). What is included in "walking" with the Torah? A third verse tells us: "You shall carry out My laws and keep My statutes so as to walk in them; I am Hashem, your God" (ibid. 18:4). "'To walk in them' — Do not free yourselves from them; you must not say, I have acquired Jewish wisdom, [now] I will go and acquire the wisdom of the other peoples [of the world]" (*Rashi*). Put in this light, we can understand why the metaphor for studying the Torah is walking, because it conveys the idea of consistency; at the same time, not studying the Torah is called "if you do not listen," because "to listen" to God can mean to learn, as the Jews said, "and we will listen."

Our Sages thus encouraged us to "Delve in it [the Torah] and continue to delve in it, for everything is in it; look deeply into it; grow old and gray over it; and do not stir from it" (*Avos* 5:26). "Everything is in it" because the Torah's wisdom encompasses all other types of wisdom. This is so because its mitzvos are done with physical actions and are connected to the nature of the world. Therefore, the meaning of each mitzvah carries a unique facet of wisdom. Since the explanations of all the mitzvos were given to Moshe at Sinai and were then passed on to our Sages, our Sages clearly had a thorough knowledge of all branches of wisdom. Still, their only interest and occupation was the study of the mitzvos, and they were not interested in those forms of wisdom per se (which is why they did not author works on topics of general knowledge).

L. No diversions

The third part of listening included: We will not engage in mundane diversions. This includes the prohibition against reading corrupt or mundane books and novels. The Sages ruled that when one reads such works, he transgresses this sin of, "Do not turn toward idols" (*Vayikra* 19:4), on which our Sages expounded: "Do not turn to something you have conjured on your own" (*Shabbos* 149a), or as Rashi explains that Gemara, "[Do not turn] to those things that you make with the thoughts of your heart, in the cavity of your [heart]." (See also *Orach Chaim* 307:16. This is besides the prohibition of sitting in a "session of scorners" and the fact that these publications incite the *yetzer hara*.)

M. Restricting our thoughts

And the fourth part was: We will restrict our thoughts. The Rambam elaborates:

> *Not only is it forbidden to think about actual idol worship, but it is also forbidden to stray after any thought that might cause someone to uproot any of the foundations of the Torah. We are warned not to entertain such thoughts, and we must not direct our minds to such thoughts, nor should we be drawn to the heart's musings. For man's judgment is limited, and not all minds are capable of attaining the clear truth. If everyone would follow whatever their hearts think of, they would destroy the world because of their limited intelligence. How so? Sometimes they may stray after idol worship, or sometimes they will think about the unity of the Creator — perhaps He is [One], perhaps not; what is above, what is below, what was before, and what will be afterward. [Other times they make think] about prophecy — perhaps it is true, perhaps it is not. Or [they may think] about the Torah — perhaps it is from Heaven, perhaps not. [Unlearned people] do not possess the values needed for judging such matters [in a way that] would lead to a clear knowledge of the truth. Consequently, [one can easily] arrive at heresy. About this the Torah warned, "You must not probe after your heart and after your eyes, after which you [tend] to stray" (Bamidbar 15:39). Meaning, do not be lured by your feeble minds to think that you can reach the truth on your own. So said our Sages: "'After your heart' — this refers to heresy; 'and after your eyes' — this refers to immorality" (Berachos 12b).*
>
> *— Rambam, Hilchos Avodas Kochavim 2:3*

Thus, the pledge "we will listen" was not simply a practicality to enable "we will do." Listening to God means more than finding out how to fulfill the mitzvos; it means we will not stray after our own thoughts in any way, but we will listen only to the words of the Torah.

N. Devoted thoughts – thoughts of devotion

Why did the Jews commit to restricting their thoughts? Because the Exodus demanded it of them. After saying, "You must not probe after your heart," Scripture continues: "I am Hashem, your God, Who took you out of the land of Egypt" (*Bamidbar* 15:41). God, in effect, told us, "When I took you out of Egypt, you became My slaves and you must therefore be completely subservient to Me." We must therefore subjugate all the potentials of our hearts and minds to the Master, may He be blessed. These verses (which are in the portion of *tzitzis*) form the very appropriate conclusion to *Krias Shema* because they too affirm our acceptance of the yoke of Heaven.

With the above, we can understand why Israel were given two crowns for saying "we will do and we will listen," for they are two separate commitments: "We are willing to do whatever He commands us, and we will think only of what He allows us to think." These are two unique qualities — crowns — that set us apart from the heretics and the nations of the world.

O. Wholehearted mitzvos

Perhaps there is one more lesson that we may learn from "we will do": that when we do a mitzvah, we should do it wholeheartedly, even if we have not yet "heard" and fully grasped its significance or importance. As Rabbi Yitzchak in the Midrash says:

> *Scripture tells you that if a person does a mitzvah, he should do it with a whole heart, for if Reuven had known that the Holy One would write about him, "Reuven heard [this] and he saved him from their hands" (Bereishis 37:21), he would have carried [Yosef] on his shoulders to his father; and had Aharon known that the Holy One would write about him, "he will also be coming out to greet you, and will see you and will be happy in his heart" (Shemos 4:14), he would have gone out toward him with tambourines and dancing; and had Boaz known that the Holy One would write about*

him, "And he passed her parched grain" (Rus 2:14), he would have fed her fattened calves.
—Rus Rabbah 5:6

Now, even though all three people mentioned in this Midrash gained much merit for what they did (Aharon, for example, merited wearing the *choshen*/breastplate over his heart), nevertheless they did not realize the significance of their actions — the "we will hear" of the verses — represented by what the Torah was to write about each one. People usually do not know at first the value of their deeds. Still, we have learned that whatever mitzvos we do should be done with all our might. This, too, is included in "'we will do' before 'we will listen.'"

P. Rus and Orpah

The difference between Rus and Orpah is an instructive example of the difference between a half-hearted mitzvah and a wholehearted one. They both wanted to do the same thing, except that one had strong will and the other had weak will. Our Sages teach that both were descendants of Eglon, king of Moav. They had rejected royalty to follow Naomi, a poor, pitiful widow, and to convert to Judaism. Still, when Naomi discouraged them from continuing, Orpah parted ways and returned to her nation (and to her gods), while Rus "clung to her" (*Rus* 1:14).

What became of them? Rus married into the tribe of Yehudah — through Boaz — and her descendants included David, the anointed king of Israel who lavished songs and praises to God. This is the David who, as a youth, was willing to gave his life to sanctify the Name of Heaven by challenging the dreaded Philistine, Golyas.

And what came of Orpah? Orpah's fall was shocking: on the very first night after parting from Naomi, she became loose (as our Sages expounded in *Rus Rabbah* 2:20). And she, too, had a descendant. His name was Golyas.

She had walked forty steps with Naomi, and for this noble act she received the merit that this descendant would stand against the Jews for forty days. Another opinion is that she had walked four *mil*, which gave her the merit to be the matriarch of four mighty warriors.

Golyas was the opposite of David. While David sang praises to God, Golyas disgraced "the battalions of the Living God" (*I Shmuel* 17:26) during those forty days "earned" by Orpah.

Of Rus it is written, "[Naomi] saw that [Rus] was determined to go with her" (*Rus* 1:18). Rationally, Rus had no reason to hope that Naomi would ever be able to help her. But Rus had attained the level of "we will do before we will listen," so she negated herself and accepted the yoke of Heaven upon herself. It is no coincidence that we learn the laws of conversion to Judaism from her example, for she displayed the very quality that "converted" the Jews to become the People of the Torah. And it is certainly no coincidence that we read the book named after her, the book of *Rus*, on Shavuos, the holiday of the Giving of the Torah, for her story is the best example of how we should all accept the Torah.

"We will do and we will listen!"

CHAPTER FIFTEEN

The Path to Receiving the Torah

A. The Real Answer

"In distress you called out, and I released you" (*Tehillim* 81:8). This happened in Egypt, when the Jews were in distress, so they called out to God: "They cried out, and their pleas that stemmed from their hard labor went up to God" (*Shemos* 2:23). "And I released you," said the Holy One — I took them out of there.

But this was still not when He really answered their call, for the verse (*Tehillim* 81:8) continues: "I answered you — when you called privately — with a thunderous reply." When was this? When was there a thunderous reply? At the Giving of the Torah! And why was the Giving of the Torah the true answer to their call and not the Exodus? Because when they cried out in distress, they were not merely asking for a reprieve from their taskmasters, they were beseeching God because they realized that "God is not with us, that is why these misfortunes have befallen us" (see *Devarim* 31:17). Jews know that the true cause of all their misfortunes is the concealment of God's presence. So the only way to bring an end to misfortune is repentance: "When you are persecuted and all these things befall you, you will then return to Hashem, your God" (*Devarim* 4:30). The Jews in Egypt were calling out, "I will go and return to my first husband" (*Hoshea* 2:9); we want to draw near to Hashem. Only that closeness would fulfill what they were really missing.

B. Beautiful souls

But there is only one way to draw closer to God: with His Torah, for God and the Torah are one. "Take words with you and return to Hashem" (ibid. 14:3). Thus God only fully answered them at the Giving of the Torah, when their closeness to Him was restored.

From the depths of their souls, the Jews in Egypt cried out: "Draw me [to You], we will run after you!" (*Shir HaShirim* 1:4). It may have seemed that they were crying because of their suffering from servitude, but, in fact, their hearts were pleading to receive the Torah. This yearning came from the beauty that is at the core of every Jew: "'I am black, yet beautiful' (ibid. v. 5); I am black in my deeds, yet I am beautiful in the deeds of my forefathers" (*Shemos Rabbah* 23:10). The Jews inherited certain qualities from the forefathers: they are compassionate, shy, and generous (see *Yevamos* 79a; these qualities also correspond to Torah from Yaakov, *avodah* [Divine service] from Yitzchak, and *gemillus chassadim* [acts of kindness] from Avraham). Above all, they inherited an inner sense and striving for truth. Thus "they are believers, sons of believers" (*Shabbos* 97a). The underlying request, then, of the Jews in Egypt was for Torah and a bond with God; therefore, "I answered you ... with a thunderous reply" (*Tehillim* 81:8) — for that was the real response to their call.

C. Humility

It is not enough, however, to reach an elevated status of spirituality; it must be maintained by remaining humble. After the Jews received God's blessing, they had to remember their past, remember that God is within them, and remember that He is watching them. But at the Waters of Strife they stumbled and wondered, "Is Hashem among us or not?" (*Shemos* 17:7). Having the Divine Presence among them, and having Him give them all their provisions, should have made them humble; instead, they became proud. They forgot that it was "Not because you are more numerous than all the nations did Hashem desire you and choose you, for you are the smallest of all the nations" (*Devarim* 7:7). They forgot that God chose us because of our innate modesty: "Said the Holy One to Israel: I desired you because even when I bestow greatness upon you, you minimize yourselves. For example, I gave greatness to Avraham, and he said (*Bereishis* 18:27), 'but I am dust and ashes'" (*Chullin* 89a). My teacher, R' Yitzchak Greenburg *zt"l*, explained that whenever Avraham was rescued by God, he would look at what he would have been if not for God's mercy on him: the kings he fought against would have turned him to "dust," and Nimrod would have reduced him to "ashes." In his eyes, he was "dust and ashes."

D. The path for all individuals

Indeed, the same order for climbing and serving God applies to all individuals. This is the significance of the word "Selah" (which often means, "forever") in the verse, "I answered you ... with a thunderous reply... Selah" (*Tehillim* 81:8). Any Jew who wishes to grow closer to God must go through the process of yearning, revelation, and maintaining humility. With this approach we can also understand the continuation of the chapter, "Listen, My people, I will attest to you .... There shall be no strange god within you .... I am Hashem, your God, Who raised you from the land of Egypt" (ibid. vs. 9-11). That is, always remember your past and God's providence that was revealed to you. "I am Hashem, your God, Who raised you from the land of Egypt; open your mouth wide and I will fill it" (ibid. v. 11). Our Sages teach that this refers to words of Torah (*Berachos* 50a); "I will fill it" with words of Torah. The purpose of the Exodus was to generate a desire in the Jews for the Torah, and to make them into a receptacle worthy of receiving the Torah. So open your mouth wide and then I will fill it just as at the Giving of the Torah. Every individual must first open his mouth before God will fill it; first he must perfect his character traits and purify his heart of all desires and cravings until his only desire is to be close to God, then God will grant him that closeness. But then he must still be careful not to become haughty from the good that God bestowed upon him or because of the Divine Presence and the Torah that is within him. He should always remind himself of his origins, for then his heart will remain faithful to God.

CHAPTER SIXTEEN

Good Character Traits

A. Look at the difference

The Holy One, Blessed is He..., [sent] Moshe to Israel and Bilam to the nations. Yet look at the difference between the prophets of Israel and [Bilam]: The prophets of Israel warn Israel to [avoid] sin, as is written, "Son of Man, I have appointed you a sentinel [for the House of Israel]" (Yechezkel 3:17); but [Bilam] made a breach [that invited sin] in order to annihilate a people from the world. Moreover, all the prophets were compassionate toward Israel and to the nations, for Yirmiyah (48:36) says, "My heart moans for Moab like flutes"; and Yechezkel (27:2)

says, "Now you, Son of Man, take up a lament for Tyre." But this cruel person [Bilam] arose to uproot an entire nation for no reason.
— Bamidbar Rabbah 20:1

B. Character traits are the roots of all action

Why did Bilam, who was a prophet, act so wickedly? Because he possessed bad character traits, and it is character traits that ultimately direct all action:

When there are bad character traits in a person, he cannot fulfill the Torah and the mitzvos, and even when he does do them, it is not for the sake of Heaven; it is a great burden. About him it is said, "A golden ring in the snout of a pig" (Mishlei 11:22), for his impurity is still within him and, as our Sages said, "If one merits, his Torah becomes an elixir for life, but if he does not merit, then it becomes a death potion for him" (Yoma 72b).
— R' Chaim Vital, Shaarei Kedushah, Part I, Gate 2

C. An inheritance of good traits

God gave us His Torah because of our good character traits. Our forefathers acquired these traits through their *avodas Hashem* and then bequeathed them to us. These traits made us most suited for receiving the Torah. God had sworn to them that He would be God to them and their offspring, as is written, "Avraham will, after all, become a great and mighty nation, and all the nations of the earth will be blessed through him. For I have known him [closely], because he directs his sons and his household after him, that they keep the way of Hashem by performing righteousness and justice" (*Bereishis* 18:18-19). And it is written, "Not because you are more numerous than all the nations did Hashem desire you and choose you, for you are the smallest of all the nations. Rather, out of Hashem's love for you, and because He kept the oath that He swore to your forefathers,

Hashem took you out with mighty force and redeemed you from the house of slavery" (*Devarim* 7:7-8). Our Sages thus said, "There are three signs of this nation: they are compassionate, shy, and generous" (*Yevamos* 79a).

D. Signs of a nation

These signs are so ingrained in the descendants of Avraham, Yitzchak, and Yaakov that David was able to use them to determine that the Givonites were not of the Children of Israel: "The king called the Givonites and said to them. The Givonites were not of the Children of Israel, but from the remnant of the Amorite" (*II Shmuel* 21:2). The end of the verse does not seem to follow its beginning (the verse begins by saying that David said something to the Givonites, but it does not continue with what he said; instead, it continues with the status of the Givonites). Our Sages, however, explained the passage very well (in *Yevamos* 79b): At first David wanted to appease the Givonites for their claim against the House of Shaul with money or something else, but they refused and reverted to their cruel nature. They demanded instead that seven of Shaul's sons be given to them and they would hang them (as recounted there, v. 6). Based on this, David determined that the Givonites cannot be truly Jewish: "They demonstrated that they possessed the trait of cruelty, which shows that they were not from the offspring of Avraham Avinu and were not worthy of being attached to Israel. David therefore decreed that they may not [marry] into the community. He said: There are three signs for this nation [of Israel]: they are compassionate, shy, and generous. Whoever has these three signs is worthy of our attachment" (*Rashi, II Shmuel* 21:2).

E. Disciples of Avraham and disciples of Bilam

Even Bilam, in his words about the unique character of the Jewish people, grudgingly admitted that they possessed these unique qualities, which were passed down from their ancestors:

"From [their] origins I see them as [firm as] rocks, and perceive them [emanating] from hills. They are a people who dwell alone and they are not reckoned among the nations" (*Bamidbar* 23:9), and Rashi explains, "'I see them as [firm as] rocks, and perceive them [emanating] from hills' — through their Fathers and Mothers."

The Sages taught:

> *Whoever has the following three traits is among the disciples of our forefather Avraham; and [whoever has] three different traits is among the disciples of the wicked Bilam. Those who have a good eye, a humble spirit, and a meek soul are among the disciples of our forefather Avraham. Those who have an evil eye, an arrogant spirit, and a greedy soul are among the disciples of the wicked Bilam.*
>
> — *Mishnah, Avos 5:22*

With some reflection we can see how the three "signs" of the Jewish people — "they are compassionate, shy, and generous" — correspond to the three traits mentioned in the Mishnah: Compassionate corresponds to "good eye"; shy corresponds to "humble spirit"; and generous to "meek soul."

F. Levels of refinement

Good character traits, then, are the fundamental conditions that made Israel suited for receiving the Torah. Having those qualities, however, are not on-or-off states — there are many levels within each character trait. The more an individual perfects his character traits, the more he increases his capacity for Torah wisdom and its mitzvos. The spiritual level of each person — from the lowest level to the level of *ruach hakodesh* and prophecy — depends on his level of character refinement. Consequently, "Torah is even greater than priesthood or royalty; for royalty is acquired along with thirty prerogatives, and the priesthood with twenty-four [gifts], but the Torah is acquired by means of forty-eight qualities" (*Avos* 6:6).

Similarly there are specific qualities necessary for the gift of prophecy: "The Divine Presence only dwells on someone who is wise, mighty, and wealthy" (*Shabbos* 92a). The Rambam elaborates:

> *Prophecy can only come upon [someone who is] very wise; mighty in his [use of his] character traits; and who does not allow his yetzer to prevail over him in any matter of the world. Rather, he always uses his mind to overcome his yetzer. He must be someone whose thinking is logical and straight. And, [in addition to all these qualities,] he [should be] of sound body [so that] when he enters the "Orchard" and he dwells on those sublime matters, his mind will be prepared to fathom and understand.*
>
> *He will continuously sanctify himself and separate himself from the paths of the rest of the people who walk in the darkness of time. He will motivate and teach himself to avoid any thoughts of idle matters, or of the vanities of time and its schemes. Instead, his mind is always directed upward.*
>
> *— Rambam, Yesodei HaTorah 7:1*

The Sages also taught that "The Divine Presence does not dwell [upon a person when he is] in a state of sadness, laziness, laughter, or frivolity. Rather, [it dwells] only through the joy of a mitzvah" (*Shabbos* 30b).

G. How could Bilam be a prophet?

We may wonder, though, how did Bilam — who did not possess any of these qualities — attain prophecy? How could someone who had "an arrogant spirit, a greedy soul, and an evil eye" (and other detestable traits recorded in *Avodah Zarah* 4b) be a prophet?

One approach is that his visions were not true prophecy, for the Sages said, "[Bilam] was not worthy of *ruach hakodesh*" (*Bamidbar Rabbah* 20:12). Rashi, as well, writes, "The words of Bilam were not uttered because the *Shechinah* rested upon him, but, [as Scripture describes it], 'He lies down and [then it is] revealed to him' (*Bamidbar* 24:4), similar to 'A message surreptitiously reached me' (*Iyov* 4:12); the [gentile prophets] hear [God's message] through a medium" (*Rashi, Shemos* 33:17).

Another approach is as the Ramban writes in several places (for instance, in his commentary to *Bamidbar* 22:31) that Bilam was essentially a sorcerer who was temporarily shown visions one level below true prophecy. Why did he merit even that level? For the sake of Israel's glory: God wanted to show His special love toward Israel, so He caused a wicked anti-Semite to bless the Jews. Even those visions were beyond what he was worthy of, so he could not maintain this level, and he later returned to his former level of being a sorcerer.

H. Character is what really counts

But Bilam misused the special gift he received and he tried using it to "curse an entire nation that had not done anything against him" (*Bamidbar Rabbah* 20:14). This was despite the fact that he knew that God did not want him to curse Israel, and despite all the warnings and impediments that God had set in his path. He could have achieved true greatness, but instead he had an ignoble end.

The reason his gift of semi-prophecy did not help him was because he had never prepared himself for that calling; he had never refined his character. We see, then, that with all his extra wisdom and Divine Inspiration, the gift itself turned against him and crushed him — because he harnessed all the power of this spiritual gift to carry out the dictates of his negative character. If beforehand he was quick to curse, now he would curse in the most powerful way possible. This is not surprising, for "whoever is greater than his friend, his *yetzer* [*hara*] is greater than his [friend's as well]" (*Succah* 52a). Whoever is truly great — because of his own efforts — can counter his mighty *yetzer hara* because his *yetzer tov* is also greater. But someone who is not truly great — someone who did not work at becoming great and only received it as a gift — has a *yetzer hara* that is indeed much greater than his friend's, yet his *yetzer hatov* is just as small as ever, so evil easily overcomes him.

This is the underlying difference between the prophets of Israel and Bilam: the prophets of Israel reached that position through hard work and self-preparation; they had to purify themselves and acquire noble character traits. Because of their good character, they used whatever talents and powers they possessed to guide others along the good path of life; and they were willing to do this for any human, including non-Jews, for all humans were created in the Divine image. But Bilam, who lacked good character, followed his bad character to do the most evil acts.

I. A lesson for all

The Midrash at the head of this chapter together with the Mishnah in Avos teaches a lesson for all on the importance of self-refinement. The Sages, in effect, are saying: "See what you will look like if you do not perfect yourself and prepare yourself to study the Torah. With the 'three different traits' you may become a 'disciple of the wicked Bilam.'" On the other hand, when one develops the three good traits he is a disciple of Avraham Avinu. And lest anyone think that good character traits are not essential — that they do not determine what sort of soul one has — and are reserved for the extra pious, the Mishnah continues:

> *How are the disciples of our forefather Avraham different from the disciples of the wicked Bilam? The disciples of our forefather Avraham enjoy [the fruits of their good deeds] in this world and inherit the World to Come.... But the disciples of the wicked Bilam inherit Gehinnom and descend to the well of destruction.*
>
> — *Avos 5:22*

This Mishnah gives us a sense of the true value of acquiring good traits. Once we know that only the disciples of Avraham "enjoy [the fruits of their good deeds] in this world and inherit the World to Come" we will not err about the importance of good traits.

J. Why does the Shechinah not rest upon wicked people?

For the remainder of the chapter we will examine the nature of Bilam's prophecy in greater depth. In section G, we raised the question of, "How could Bilam be a prophet?" and we offered a few solutions. We will now discuss that topic in sharper detail.

> *God said to Bilam, "You must not go with them. You must not curse the people, for they are blessed. Bilam arose in the morning and said to Balak's dignitaries, "Go [back] to your country, for Hashem has refused to let me go with you"*
>
> *— Bamidbar 22:12-13*
>
> *Bilam responded and said to Balak's servants, "Even if Balak gives me his whole palace full of silver and gold, I would not be able to violate the word of Hashem, my God."*
>
> *— Ibid. v. 18*
>
> *Bilam lifted up his eyes and saw Israel dwelling according to its tribes.*
>
> *— Ibid. 24:2*

Rashi, based on the Sages, shows how these verses highlight the three traits of Bilam:

> *"'[Hashem has refused] to let me go with you' — but [only] with princes greater than you. This tells us that he was of arrogant spirit and he did not want to divulge that he was under the control of [God]" (Rashi, Bamidbar 22:13).*
>
> *"'Full of silver and gold' — this tells us that he had a greedy soul and was covetous of the wealth of others" (v. 18).*
>
> *"'Bilam lifted up his eyes' — he wished to cast an evil eye upon them. Thus you have his three traits: an evil eye, arrogance, and greed, which we have mentioned above."*
>
> *— (Rashi ibid. 24:2).*

What is Rashi trying to teach us? Is he trying to explain that these verses are the sources for the Mishnah in Avos? That cannot be, because Rashi's approach in his commentary to *Chumash* was to comment only when there is a textual difficulty in a verse, and he would not have mentioned a related topic unless it shed light on the verse he was elucidating. Besides, this comment about the "three bad traits" belongs here no more than it does in the passages that discussed Avraham's life — to show the source for the "three good traits," yet Rashi did not mention the Mishnah in *Avos* there.

Rashi, however, seems to be completing a thought he had raised earlier:

> *And if you ask: Why did the Holy One let His Shechinah rest upon a wicked heathen? It was in order that the heathens should have no excuse to say, "If we had prophets, we would have changed for the better," so He set up prophets for them. Yet they broke down the [moral] fence of the world, because at first they were fenced in against immoral living, but this man [Bilam] counseled them to freely offer themselves to harlotry.*
>
> — *Rashi, Bamidbar 22:5*

The question Rashi is raising is that it should be impossible for a wicked person to be a prophet, for R' Yochanan said, "The Holy One allows His *Shechinah* to rest only upon someone who is mighty, wealthy, wise, and humble" (*Nedarim* 38a). The requirements of a prophet demand that he be a righteous person. For example, the requirement of being "mighty" means, as the Rambam explains, that he must be "mighty in his character traits"; that is, someone who is in control of all his traits.[1] How, then, did the *Shechinah* rest upon the wicked Bilam?

---

1. The commentators of the Rambam ask that the Gemara (both in *Nedarim* and in *Shabbos* 92a) implies that the requirement that the prophet be "mighty" and "wealthy" is meant literally. The *Kesef Mishneh* answers this question based on the *Rosh's* interpretation of that Gemara. The *Rosh* understood that the Gemara was describing only people who receive the *Shechinah's* presence on a regular basis, but people who merited receiving the *Shechinah* temporarily do not have to be literally mighty and wealthy. The *Kesef Mishneh* suggests that the Rambam was not discussing the requirements of a permanent prophet but those of a temporary prophet, that even a temporary prophet must be at least "wealthy" in the sense of being happy with his lot and "mighty" by being someone "who subdues his personal inclination" (*Avos* 4:1), as the Rambam discusses in the seventh chapter of his *Shemonah Perakim.*

To this, Rashi answers that in this case the *Shechinah* did dwell on a wicked heathen "in order that the heathens should have no excuse." In other words, this episode showed what happens when the *Shechinah* dwells on a wicked person and why it does not dwell on one: it causes more harm than good. And so that we would understand why this is so, Rashi notes that Bilam had three negative traits. This explains why the *Shechinah* does not dwell on a wicked person: he does not possess the three good traits (this is why if somebody develops the opposite of these good traits, he becomes a "disciple of the wicked Bilam").

K. "Prophets of truth and righteousness"

Bilam did not retain his status of semi-prophet — though God does not usually retract His gifts[2] — because he had never really changed. Had Bilam put in the effort to perfect himself, he would have retained it, but since he followed his traits, they caused him to be removed from the world.

There are thus two reasons why having a good character is the precondition of prophecy: The first is that bad character traits form a barrier between the person and God and thereby block the reception of the Divine message (as elaborated by the Rambam in *Hilchos Yesodei HaTorah* and in Chapter Seven of his *Shemonah Perakim*). And the second is that, as we have discovered in the works of the Sages, if a prophet has bad character traits, he will put his prophecy to negative use. If one's traits are good, he will use his power for the benefit of mankind, but if they are bad, he will use his power for the detriment of mankind. Because

2. There are two sources for this concept. The Sages taught: "When the Holy One confers greatness upon a person, He does so for [that person and for] his children and children's children" (*Megillah* 13b). The second source is from the Gemara's comment about the miracle that happened to R' Chanina. Heaven gave R' Chanina one of the golden legs set aside for his "table" in Heaven, but R' Chanina returned it because he did not want to consume the reward of his afterlife in this world. The Gemara comments that the fact that Heaven took back the golden leg was a greater miracle than when it was given, for "[Heaven] surely gives, but they don't take anything back!" (*Taanis* 25a).

prophecy is so potent, it cannot be given to someone who will only use it to become even more evil. The proof for all this is Bilam's behavior — he would have cursed and consumed a nation, had the Holy One not forced him to say something good.

The blessing recited before the reading of the *haftarah* now takes on fresh meaning. The blessing reads, "Blessed are You... Who has chosen good prophets and was pleased with their words that were uttered with truth." What are "good" prophets? Are there bad ones? They are "good" when they have good character traits, and only they are the ones whom God "has chosen." Furthermore, bad traits are forces of evil and falsehood, so when someone is steeped in them, he cannot see the truth. Consequently, if someone with bad traits were to receive a message from God, he would distort the message — the words of God that would come out of his mouth would not be "uttered with truth." In this, as well, Bilam is the example of a distorting prophet, for the Holy One told him, "You must not go with them" (*Bamidbar* 22:12) and reiterated, "You must not curse the people, for they are blessed." Yet Bilam interpreted the message to mean, "'[Hashem has refused to allow me] to go with you' — but only with princes greater than you" (*Rashi*, ibid. v. 13). His arrogant mind distorted the word of Hashem. On the other hand, God is "pleased with the words" of the "good prophets," for they are "uttered with truth."

The blessing concludes: "Blessed are you, Hashem, Who chooses... the prophets of truth and righteousness." The wording of the blessing reflects the two advantages of prophets who have good traits: "prophets of truth" corresponds to clear reception of God's words, without any barriers; and "righteousness" corresponds to using the prophecy for the good (which is the second reason given above).

L. Bilam could not fathom the greatness of the forefathers

"Something that a person is not responsible for, is not on his mind" (*Shavuos* 41b); people tend to think only of matters to which they can relate. This is why Bilam could not fathom the great stature of the forefathers and thought that he could make himself superior to them. When the Holy One caused Bilam's donkey to stop three times to hint to him that he would not be able to curse Israel, for they descend from "the three patriarchs" (*Rashi, Bamidbar* 22:25), Bilam ignored the hint. Instead, he said, "I have set up the seven altars and offered up a bull and a ram on each altar" (ibid. 23:4). "I have set up seven altars is not written here, but 'I have set up *the* seven altars.' [Bilam] said to Him: The ancestors of these people [together] built before You seven altars, but I alone have built altars equal to all of them" (*Rashi* ad loc.). He did not understand that their offerings stemmed from a good source — to do the Creator's will — and that they were following God, whereas his motives stemmed from an evil source. His seven altars were seven abominations, for all were designed to betray God's will. Thus, "God's rage was aroused because he was going [willingly]" (*Bamidbar* 22:22). Bilam was the exact opposite of the forefathers.

One may counter that Bilam did respect Israel's ancestry, for he said, "From their origins I see them as [firm as] rocks" (ibid. 23:9), but that was only later, after the Holy One forced him to bless Israel. As Rashi wrote, "'God chanced upon Bilam' — this is an expression of... something shameful... only to show how dear Israel was to Him" (*Rashi* ibid. v. 4).

CHAPTER SEVENTEEN

Love of Peace

A. Is the need for peace self-evident or not?

We have learned: "The world endures on three things — justice, truth, and peace" (*Avos* 1:18). Why is peace so important? We would think that it is because of the comfort it brings us — we prefer peace over strife. But if that is the case, why does the Torah have to repeatedly admonish us to promote peace? After all, the Torah is usually terse about anything that is self-evident. Or, we could ask the opposite: If the need for peace is so obvious, why is it so lacking in the world? Our Sages even record that "[Before Man was created,] Peace said, 'He should not be created, for he is full of strife' " (*Bereishis Rabbah* 8:5)!

B. Seek peace for its own sake

We have also learned, "Be among the disciples of Aharon, loving peace, and pursuing peace, loving people, and bringing them closer to Torah (*Avos* 1:12). From there we see that it is not enough to be peaceful, but one must love peace. We are to seek peace for its own sake and not for the comfort it gives us. This would make our attitude toward peace similar to the Rambam's exhortation to "Do [love] truth because it is truth" (*Rambam, Hilchos Teshuvah* 10:2); we may similarly say, "Love peace because it is peace." Indeed, of both it is written, "Love truth and peace" (*Zechariah* 8:19). For if we are interested only in our own comfort, then we are merely loving ourselves, not peace. If our love of peace depends on our comfort, then we may lose it at some point, for "Any love that depends on a specific cause, when that cause is gone, the love is gone; but if it does not depend on a specific cause, it will never cease" (*Avos* 5:19).

For example, if Korach would have possessed the trait of loving peace, he never would have become jealous and he never would have launched a dispute against Moshe, because a good trait can counteract a bad one. Even a greedy person will control his desire in the presence of others — if he has the trait of shame. People almost always exchange one character trait for another: one person may give away money in order to gain honor; another will degrade himself and sell his honor to make money — it all depends on the intensity of the traits that are active in the person at that time. Therefore, if one's appreciation of peace "depends on a specific cause," such as its convenience, then one's trait of jealousy may at some point be more "convenient" than peace and will override it. But when somebody loves peace itself, and it is not for the comfort it gives, then it can never be nullified by another trait.

C. Restore peace between others

Furthermore, if our interest in peace was only because of the convenience of having it, then it would be limited to relationships that involve one's self, and there would be no duty to bring peace between others. Our attitude would be, "I want to live in peace with others." Yet we know that Aharon loved and brought peace between others — between man and man and between man and wife (see *Avos D'Rabi Nosson*, Ch. 12) — so the call to "Be among the disciples of Aharon" means to restore peace between others, even when there is no particular benefit for the one who pursues it.

How can we acquire this trait of loving peace for its own sake? One suggestion that may help is to train ourselves to be concerned for the welfare of others, for "the more charity, the more peace" (*Avos* 2:8). This works because loving peace really means loving people, which explains the continuation of that Mishnah: "Be among the disciples of Aharon, loving peace, and pursuing peace, loving people, and bringing them closer to Torah (ibid. 1:12). Accordingly, pursuing peace is included in the mitzvah of "You shall love your fellowman as yourself" (*Vayikra* 19:18).

D. Put your friend first

Another suggestion for developing love of peace is to elevate your friend over yourself. When we put our friends first, we focus on them instead of on ourselves. We learn this from the angels, as described in *Avos D'Rabi Nosson*:

> *How do we know that they fear each other, honor each other, and that they are more humble than humans? For when they open their mouths to sing [praises of the Holy One], one says to his friend, "You start, for you are greater than me," and the other one [responds,] "[No,] you start, for you are greater than me." This is the opposite of humans: One says to his friend, "I am bigger than you," and the other replies, "[No,] I am bigger than you." Another opinion is that there are many groups [of angels], and each group says to the other, "You start for you are greater than us," as is written, "And one would call to another and say" (Yeshayah 6:3).*
>
> *— Avos D'Rabi Nosson, Ch. 12, s.v. Rodef shalom*

Why do the angels offer one another to start singing first? What difference would it make if one began before the other? The answer is that obviously the angels would not be offended if some would begin before the others, for they are all obligated to sing to God. But they offer one another to be the first because they exist in a state of true peace, and that is exactly what peace is: to be concerned about the other fellow. When one person says to another, "I am greater than you," he tears down the foundation of peace between them and they become "full of strife." But when somebody places his friend first, he more than promotes peace, he creates it.

E. Pursuing peace honors God

Peace is so important that we are permitted to do certain things that are normally forbidden in order to restore or maintain peace (but only when there is no more straightforward alternative). For example, in some cases it is permissible to say a falsehood in order to maintain peace;[1] we are allowed to use God's Name in blessing our fellowman;[2] and the Torah tells us to erase the Name of God in the water given to the *sotah* (a wife who was suspected of adultery).[3] These are permissible because all these activities actually honor God, for one of His Names is "Peace" (*Shabbos* 10b), and the *Shechinah* dwells only where peace is found, as is written, "[God] has become King in Yeshurun whenever the total number of the people is gathered [and] the tribes of Israel are together" (*Devarim* 33:5); "When they gather together in one band and there is peace between them, [only] then is He their King, but not when there is dissension among them" (*Rashi* ad loc.).

We can understand the connection between peace and honoring God if we keep in mind that there is a cycle: the more one recognizes God, the more humble he becomes, and the more humble one is, the more he will recognize God. When some-

---

1. See *Yevamos* 65b and *Sefer Chassidim* 426.
2. See *Berachos* 54a.
3. See *Shabbos* 116a.

body submits himself to his friend because he sees his friend as someone who is closer to God than he is, that increases God's glory. "Who may sojourn in Your tent...? One who... honors those who fear Hashem" (*Tehillim* 15:4). If the reason I honor somebody is because he fears Hashem, then I am really honoring God.

Or I may honor a friend because I recognize that he is one of God's creatures, as in the phrase "he who honors the creatures" (*Avos* 4:1). Here, too, I am really honoring God, for He is my friend's Creator. Our Sages thus said, "Who is honored? He who honors the creatures [others]" (ibid.), and they derived it from the verse, "For those who honor Me I will honor" (*I Shmuel* 2:30). They specifically used the description of "the creatures," because when people show respect to those "creatures" it is considered giving honor to God ("those who honor Me").

F. The humble are a song

When the angels give honor to one another by allowing others to start their song first, they thereby "proclaim His holiness" as one, because they "lovingly grant permission to one another to sanctify the One Who formed them" (*Siddur, Shacharis*); this is in itself a song to the Creator.

Moshe and Aharon followed this exact pattern. When God sent them to talk to the people, "They showed respect to each other, and they said to each other, 'You speak,' and the [Divine] Utterance would go forth from both of them" (*Rashi, Shemos* 12:3, from the *Mechilta*).

Similarly, Pinchas and Calev, the spies sent by Yehoshua, needed to hide from their pursuers, and "The woman [Rachav] had taken the two men and had hidden him" (*Yehoshua* 2:4). But they were two men, so why does the verse say that she hid "him" — what happened to the other one?

> *Pinchas said to her, "I am a Kohen, and a Kohen is like an angel, as is written, 'For the lips of the Kohen shall safeguard knowledge... for he is an agent [malach, angel]*

of Hashem' (Malachi 2:7), and an angel, if he wishes, he can be seen, but if he wishes, he can be invisible." So she only hid Calev.

— Yalkut Shimoni, Yehoshua §8

Pinchas had recognized God to such an extent that the *Shechinah* dwelled upon him and he had completely negated himself. It was as though he did not exist, and he was able — at will — to become literally invisible. Ironically, the greater someone is, the less visible he is; and smaller one is, the more visible he is. This may be compared to the difference between fruit-bearing trees and trees that don't bear fruit: "They say to the trees of food, 'Why does your voice not travel?' They said to them, 'We don't need to — our fruit testify for us.' They say to the barren trees, 'Why are you so noisy?' They said to them, 'If only our voices could be heard!'" (*Bereishis Rabbah* 16:3). Those who are truly great do not need to "make noise" to be important — they can be very, very quiet.

G. "We will sanctify Your Name"

The text of the *Kedushah* reads, "We will sanctify Your Name... just as they sanctify it in the highest Heaven." The order seems inverted, for the angels are not allowed to begin singing until Israel sings to God (see *Chullin* 91b). However, "just as they" is not referring to what we say, but to the manner in which we will say it. Just as they grant permission to each other, we will sanctify Your Name, for that is the essence of the song — it demonstrates that we recognize Hashem and accept His yoke. In the *Kedushah* that we say in the blessing of *Yotzer Ohr* (before the morning *Shema*) this is even more explicit: "Then they all accept upon themselves the yoke of heavenly sovereignty from one another, and lovingly grant permission to one another to sanctify the One Who formed them." That is, each one accepts upon himself the yoke of heavenly sovereignty by contemplating his own small stature compared to his friend's greatness and closeness to God — as it appears to him. Each one then gives permission to his friend to sing first, but in the end "All of them as one proclaim His holiness." This approach is supported by Tosafos (*Chagigah* 13b, s.v. *M'zei'asan shel Chayos*) who explains why there are some angels that only exist for one day. The Gemara there says that there are angels that are created every day from the sweat of *Chayos*/angels. Tosafos explains that these angels do not know the angels' custom of asking permission from one another so they rush to praise. Since they were not granted permission to sing, they are immediately eliminated, but those that did receive permission remain.

H. A dispute for the sake of Heaven

> *Any dispute that is for the sake of Heaven will have a constructive outcome; but one that is not for the sake of Heaven will not have a constructive outcome. What sort of dispute was for the sake of Heaven? The dispute between Hillel and Shammai. And which was not for the sake of Heaven? The dispute of Korach and his entire company.*
> — *Avos 5:20*

There is a famous question asked on this *Mishnah*: Why is it that concerning a dispute that is for the sake of Heaven both sides of the dispute are given: Hillel vs. Shammai; but in the dispute that is not for the sake of Heaven, the Mishnah only mentions one side: "Korach and his entire company," while Moshe is not mentioned? The answer is that indeed Moshe was not party to the dispute. In a dispute for the sake of Heaven both sides are trying to reach the truth, so both sides count. But in a dispute that is not for the sake of Heaven, such as in Korach's dispute, only one side is trying to gain something. In Korach's dispute, neither Moshe nor Aharon were trying to get anything. Moshe told "Korach and his company" that it was God's will that Aharon should be the Kohen Gadol and therefore there is nothing to complain about. Still, in his humility and because of his desire for peace, Moshe tried his best to appease the dissenters. He even sent for Dasan and Aviram to give them a chance to repent. He did this despite the fact that they had always hated Moshe and quarreled against him; they are the ones who had reported him to Pharaoh, forcing him to flee Egypt. When they scorned his invitation and their punishment was imminent, Moshe Rabbeinu, the master of all the prophets and all the scholars, exerted himself to come to them, but they still refused to repent. From Moshe's extraordinary efforts to restore peace, the Gemara learns, "From here [we learn] that one should not uphold a quarrel" (*Sanhedrin* 110a). Though it was they who started the dispute and the dispute was one sided, nevertheless Moshe worried for their welfare. When he saw that he could not help them, he turned his concern to the *shalom* and welfare of all Israel — that they should not be drawn after Korach and his company. Because belief in Moshe's prophecy is so fundamental to the Torah, and Korach's dispute was undermining this belief, Moshe requested that the dissenters should be punished — all for the sake of Israel's peace (see *Bamidbar* 16:15).

CHAPTER EIGHTEEN

The Power of Sight

A. Ayin hara on property

Seeing is not just vision. With our eyes we can affect ourselves and others, both constructively and destructively. Sight can affect property, body, and soul.

In this chapter we have assembled a list of the effects of sight, culled from our holy sources. Some of them are brought about by the one, or to the one, who looks at others; and some are what could happen to someone who is gazed upon by others.

Ayin hara, the "evil eye," on property: Our Sages taught: "It is forbidden to stand at a friend's field when its crop is fully grown" (*Bava Metzia* 107a), "so that you don't ruin it with an *ayin hara*" (*Rashi*). They also taught: "If one found a garment [that someone lost] ... he may not spread it out over a bed or a frame for his own benefit, but he may spread it out on a bed or frame if it will benefit the item. If guests came to him, he may not spread it out over a bed or frame even if it is for the item's benefit... because it will be consumed... by the evil eye [of the guests]" (*Bava Metzia* 30a).

B. Ayin hara on a person

Ayin hara can affect a person: "'Hashem will remove from you every illness' (*Devarim* 7:15). Rav said, 'This refers to the [evil] eye [that causes almost all illness].' Rav is consistent with his position elsewhere, for Rav went up to a graveyard, and did what he did. He said, 'Ninety-nine [die] from an evil eye, and one by natural causes'" (*Bava Metzia* 107b). Rashi explains that Rav knew how to whisper certain charms upon the graves, through which he was able to determine the cause for each person's death — whether it was by an evil eye or whether the person had reached his allotted time to live. Rav concluded that 99 percent of the people had died due an evil eye!

Self-ruination by possessing an *ayin hara:* "Rabbi Yehoshua says: An evil eye, the evil inclination, and hatred of other people remove a person from the world" (*Avos* 2:16). Rabbeinu Yonah explains why this is so:

> *When someone is not happy with his lot and is jealous of his friend's wealth — and he thinks to himself, "When will I be as wealthy as he?" — he harms himself and his friend. For doctors of nature have said that when one covets something that belongs to his friend, a spirit rises from that thought and consumes the items he coveted with his jealous, evil eye. He thereby consumes himself, as well, because he desired things beyond his reach.*
> — *Rabbeinu Yonah, Avos 2:16*

The self-consuming nature of having an evil eye is an apt punishment for the person who has one. An example of this is Bilam and the fate he suffered: He wished to cast an evil eye upon Israel but he was harmed instead; he became the man "with the hollow eye" (*Bamidbar* 24:3; see *Bamidbar Rabbah* 20:6 and *Midrash Talpiyos* 98).

There are even animals, such as the viper, that can harm with their sight (see *Tanchuma, Beshalach* 18 and *Midrash Talpiyos* 98). On the other hand, the *bas hayaanah* bird broods its young with its sight! And the Talmud (*Chullin* 63b) explains that the *ra'ah* bird (listed in *Devarim* 14:13) is named so because of its extraordinary ability to see (*ra'ah*) very far.

C. Damaging for the onlooker

Gazing at the air of a plague: When Sodom was being overturned, the angels said to Lot, "Do not look behind you" (*Bereishis* 19:17). The Ramban explains:

> *The rationale for the prohibition against looking [at the destruction]... is that looking at the air of a pestilence [zone], or that of other contagious diseases, can be very harmful and can lead to contracting it. Even thinking of them [can be harmful]. This is why someone who is afflicted with tzaraas is quarantined [and kept out of sight] (see Vayikra 13:46). Similarly, when people who have been bitten by a wild dog, or the like, look at water or some other reflective surface, they see the image of the damaging force [that has infected them] and they may become insane or die — as our Sages have said in Yoma (84a).... This is why Lot's wife became a pillar of salt [when she turned around to look at the destruction of Sodom] (see Bereishis 19:26); when she saw the sulfur and salt raining down on them from the sky, she began thinking of the plague and it became attached to her.*
>
> *— Ramban, Bereishis 19:17*

The Torah recounts an episode in the Desert when there was an attack of fiery snakes against Israel because they had complained about the manna. God then told Moshe what the remedy should be for those who had been bitten: "Moshe made a copper [image of a] snake and placed it on a high pole, and it was, if the snakes had bitten a man, he would then gaze at the copper snake and live" (*Bamidbar* 21:9). How did this work? The Ramban clarifies:

> *The key to this enigma, as it seems to me, is that the incidents [recorded in] the Torah are miracles within miracles: damage is repaired with the very thing that caused the damage, and illness is cured with the very thing that caused the disease. [For instance,] "Hashem instructed him about a tree. He cast it into the water and the water became sweet" (Shemos 15:25); and Elisha similarly sweetened the water with salt (see II Melachim 2:21). Now, we know that, medically, it is dangerous for someone who has been bitten by a poisonous animal to look at it or its image, so much so that those who have been bitten by a rabid dog or other rabid animals who look at water, see [in it] the image of the dog and they are [likely to] die, as is recorded in the medical texts and in the Talmud, Tractate Yoma (84a). For this reason, doctors are careful not to mention the name of the [animal] that bit [a person] in his presence, so that [the patient] will not be reminded of it and fixate on [the animal] — it may kill him....*
>
> *This being the case, Israel, who where bitten by fiery serpents, should not have been allowed to mention or even think of serpents whatsoever,[1] yet the Holy One, Blessed is He, commanded Moshe to make for them an image of a serpent — the very thing that should have been deadly for them...!*
>
> *In short, God instructed that they be healed with a dangerous item that, by nature, should have killed them. Yet they made an image and namesake of it. Then, when a*

1. *Radak* in the name of his father (*Sharashim* s.v. *Nachash* cited in R' C. D. Chavel's glosses to this Ramban): "The medical doctors said that if a person who was bitten by a snake (*nachash*) sees copper (*nechoshes*), he will die immediately. Therefore, the Holy One told Moshe to make a copper snake, and anyone who looks at it will live — contrary to the nature of the world, to magnify the miracle. -ed.

[stricken] person intentionally gazed at the copper serpent — which was an exact replica of the dangerous item — he would live. This was to inform [Israel] that it is God Who brings death and gives life.

— Ramban, Bamidbar 21:9

The Mishnah asks: "Is it the snake that kills or the snake that gives life? Rather, when Israel looked upward and submitted their hearts to their Father in Heaven, they were healed" (*Rosh Hashanah* 3:8). "Looked upward" means that they realized that their predicament was a punishment from Heaven for complaining about the manna. Once they had acknowledged that they had been ungracious to God, He healed them.

D. When it is good to be looked upon

Being looked at is not always bad. The Ramban (to *Bamidbar* 1:45) explains that the census conducted in the Desert was done by having all the Jews "counted before Moshe and Aharon, so that they would place their eyes on the [Jews] for the good, and so that they would pray for them, 'may Hashem, the God of your forefathers, increase your number a thousandfold' (cf. *Devarim* 1:11), and not decrease your numbers." Indeed, we find elsewhere that Moshe was rewarded "measure for measure" for his good eye: the Gemara (*Nedarim* 38a) teaches that the verse, "One with a good eye will be blessed" (*Mishlei* 22:9) was said of Moshe.

E. Beneficial sight

When we see our food, we are more satisfied: The Sages taught (*Yoma* 74b): "There is no comparison between one who sees and eats to one who eats without seeing. Said Rav Yosef, 'This indicates that the blind cannot become sated when they eat.' Said Abaye, 'Therefore, if someone has a meal, he should eat it only by day.' Said Rabbi Zeira, 'What is the source? "Better is what the eyes see than what is imagined" (*Koheles* 6:9).'" Furthermore, in the passage about the sin of Adam, Scripture states: "it was desirable to the eyes" (*Bereishis* 3:6). That desire led Adam to eat from the Tree of Knowledge, which was when the evil inclination entered mankind — and it all began with the eyes! From then on "The eye is never sated with seeing" (*Koheles* 1:8) and "his eye is never sated with riches" (ibid. 4:8).

F. Hazardous to the soul

Damage or benefit to the soul through seeing: The Ibn Ezra writes on the rationale for the mitzvah of "Your camp shall be holy" (*Devarim* 23:15) — the mitzvah to make sure that body waste is disposed properly — that "looking at anything repulsive to the eyes makes a negative impression on the soul."

Gazing unnecessarily at impure animals damages the soul. (The halachah to recite a blessing upon seeing an unusual animal does not contradict this, because in that case a passing glance is sufficient, whereas here we are talking about a prolonged gaze.)

Gazing at idols and their accouterments is forbidden and is damaging (see *Shabbos* 149a). This is derived from the verse, "Do not turn towards idols" (*Vayikra* 19:4).

Gazing at a wicked person is forbidden and is damaging. The Talmud (*Megillah* 28a) derives this from the comment made by the prophet Elisha to King Yehoram, son of Achav: "[I swear] that if not for the presence of Yehoshaphat, king of Yehudah, whom I respect, I would not look at you nor see you!" (*II Melachim* 3:14). There is a spirit of impurity that dwells on wicked people. Perhaps when somebody gazes at the face of a wicked person, that spirit spreads to his own face.

G. Sight in the service of the evil inclination

Seeing can arouse one's evil inclination: "Jealousy, lust, and glory remove a man from the world" (*Avos* 4:28), and all three are activated and depend on sight:

Jealousy comes by looking at something that belongs to your friend. For this reason, unless you have a particular reason for doing so, you should refrain from looking at your friend's possessions. Being curious is no excuse: curiosity is jealousy's cousin.

Lust certainly begins with sight: "You must not probe after your heart and after your eyes after which you stray" (*Bamidbar* 15:39). "The heart and the eyes are the 'spies' of the body — they act as agents for sinning: the eyes see, and the heart covets and the body commits the sin" (*Rashi*). And our Sages said, "'[He] shuts his eyes from seeing evil' (*Yeshayah* 33:15) — this is like [what] Rabbi Chiya bar Abba said, 'This refers to one who does not look at women when they are washing the laundry [and inadvertently expose themselves]'" (*Makkos* 24a). (This verse also includes refraining from looking at the shortcomings and deficiencies of other people. As Rashi wrote: "'You must not go around as a gossip-monger [*racheel*] among your people' (*Vayikra* 19:16); I say that because all those who sow discord [between people] and all who speak slander go into their friends' houses to spy out what evil they can see there, or what evil they can hear there so that they may tell it in the streets; they are called *holchei racheel* [which is similar to] *holchei rageela*, 'people who go about spying.'") Our Sages also said, "A person's *yetzer hara* only takes control over what his eyes see" (*Yalkut Shimoni, Emor* §658).

Glory also comes by sight; when someone sees that people are giving him honor, he comes to pride. Or when someone sees his own superiority in some areas, such as beauty, he can be filled with misplaced pride, as in the story recounted in the Talmud:

> *Said Shimon HaTzaddik: I never ate from the guilt-offering of a nazir who became defiled, except for once: One time a nazir came from the South, and I saw that he had beautiful eyes and he was handsome, and the locks of his hair were arranged in curls. I said to him, "My son, why did you decide to ruin your beautiful hair?" He said to me: "I was a shepherd for my father in my town; I went to fill up water from the spring, and I saw my reflection. My inclination overwhelmed me, and sought to drive me out of the world. I said to it, 'Wicked one! Why are you so full of pride over a world that does not belong to you? Over one*

that is destined to become maggots and worms? I swear, I shall shave you for the sake of Heaven!'"

— Nedarim 9b

This can be understood with the idea that haughtiness is the seat of the *yetzer hara,* and the *yetzer hara* is desire, as the Gra wrote in *Even Sheleimah.* From the above we can also see why it is harmful for a man to gaze at a mirror unnecessarily (see *Shulchan Aruch, Yoreh Deah* 156:2).

Another example of how sight incites the *yetzer hara* can be found in the following Midrash:

> *One of Rabbi Yonasan's students ran away to join [a band of decadent people].... [They tried ensnaring Rabbi Yonasan, as well, so] they said to him, "Rabbi, come and do a kindness for a bride." He went [thinking he was going to a wedding, but when he arrived,] he found them all occupied [immorally] with a certain maiden. He said to them, "Is this the way Jews behave...?" [When he saw how brazen they were,] he ran away but they chased him until he reached his door and he closed it before them. They said, "Rabbi Yonasan, go tell your mother with fanfare that you did not turn your face to look at us, for if you would have turned around to look at us, more than we were chasing after you, you would have chased after us [to be like us].*
>
> *— Koheles Rabbah 1:[8:4][25]*

We see, then, that he was spared from their terrible influence only because he had not looked at them at all.

The *Yalkut Shimoni* recounts:

> *Rabbi Masia ben Charash was once sitting in the study hall, engrossed in the Torah. His face shone like the sun, and it resembled that of the angels because he had never lifted his eyes to look at a woman. One time, the Satan passed by him and was jealous of him. The Satan said to himself, "Is it possible that a man like this never sinned?"*

He said before the Holy One, Blessed is He, "Master of the Universe! What is Rabbi Masia ben Charash before you?" He said to him, "He is a perfect tzaddik." He said before Him, "Give me permission to entice him." He said to him, "You cannot conquer him." Nevertheless, He told him to go.

[The Satan] appeared before [Rabbi Masia] in the guise of a beautiful woman the likes of which had not been in the world since the days of Naamah, the sister of Tuval Kayin (who caused the angels' error, as is written, "The sons of the nobility saw the daughters of the common people" [Bereishis 6:2]). As soon as he saw [the Satan], he turned his head [thinking it was a woman]. Again he came and stood to his left. He turned his head to the right. [Satan] moved around him from all sides. [Rabbi Masia] said to himself, "I am afraid my yetzer hara may overcome me and cause me to sin." What did that tzaddik do? He called one of his students who was attending him, and said to him, "Go bring me fire and a nail." [The student] brought nails for him and [Rabbi Masia blinded himself by] putting them in his eyes. When the Satan saw this he shuddered and fell back. The Holy One immediately called [the angel] Refael and said to him, "Go heal R' Masia ben Charash." He came and stood before him. [Refael] said to him, "I am Refael whom the Holy One sent to heal your eyes." [Rabbi Masia] responded, "Leave me; whatever was, was...." The Holy One said to him, "Go tell him that I am his guarantor that the yetzer hara will never overcome him again." He immediately healed him. From here the Sages said, "Whoever does not gaze at women, and all the more so at married women, the yetzer hara does not dominate him.

— Yalkut Shimoni, Vayechi §161

I heard from my teacher, the *tzaddik* Rabbi Eliyahu Lopian *zt"l*, that there is a tradition from our Sages that all of a person's deeds are recorded in his eyes. When the time comes for him to die, Heaven reviews everything before him, and he signs on all of it that it is accurate. This tradition was carried for centuries, well before photography and motion pictures were invented. Now that these techniques exist, it is much easier for us to envision how this could be.

"The Sages say: The height of the Angel of Death is from one end of the world to the other; from the soles of his feet to the top of his head, he is all eyes" (*Maseches Kallah* 3:1). Why does the Angel of Death need so many eyes? In light of our discussion, we may explain that the *yetzer hara* (who is also the Angel of Death, see *Bava Basra* 16a) draws most of his power from what the person looks at. One point for us to ponder is the fact that his eyes cover his entire "body," which is as long as the whole world.

H. Constructive sights for the soul

Looking at *tzitzis* assists in several important mitzvos: (a) accepting the yoke of Heaven; (b) remembering the Exodus; (c) remembering all the mitzvos and the influence of their holiness. Thus it is written, "They shall be for you as *tzitzis* [tassels], so that you see them and thereby remember all Hashem's commandments and carry them out" (*Bamidbar* 15:39). *Tzitzis* remind people of Hashem's commandments "because the numerical value of the word '*tzitzis*' is 600, and there are eight strings and five knots, so that you have 613" (*Rashi, Bamidbar* ibid.). Looking at *tzitzis* also gives one the merit to greet the *Shechinah* (see *Menachos* 43b).

Looking at the sky helps one gain fear of Heaven, as is written, "Raise your eyes on high and see Who created these things!" (*Yeshayah* 40:26). The Talmud (*Berachos* 34b) instructs that one should pray in a building that has windows. Rashi understands that this is so that the worshiper could, if need be, look through the windows to see the sky, which would help subdue him and he would concentrate better. Rabbeinu Yonah suggests that perhaps looking at light will help the person settle his mind and he will be able to concentrate properly (see also *Shulchan Aruch, Orach Chaim* 90:4).

Looking at the face of a *tzaddik* is beneficial for the soul. This probably works because the soul of the onlooker becomes attached to the spirit of holiness that hovers over the *tzaddik*. Similarly, when one looks at a wise man, he himself becomes wiser, as Rebbi said, "If I am sharper than my colleagues, it is because I saw Rabbi Meir from his back; and had I seen him from his front, I would have been even sharper, as is written (*Yeshayah* 30:20), 'Your eyes will behold your teacher'" (*Eruvin* 13b).

I. Some suggestions

(a) There are two verses that advise us on how to protect our eyes: "A clever person sees evil and hides" (*Mishlei* 22:3), and "The wise man has eyes in his head" (*Koheles* 2:14). If you are wise, then put your "eyes in your head": try to foresee danger spots — situations where your eyes may be exposed to something you should not see.

(b) Train yourself not to scan your surroundings unnecessarily. Look down as much as appropriate. The holy works advise that "one should be careful to guard the covenant of the tongue, the covenant of the skin and the covenant of the eyes" (see *Birkei Yosef, Orach Chaim* 603:2) because all three are interconnected.

(c) *Maaseh Rav* (in the name of the Gra) recommends that we pray for the spiritual safety of our eyes before going anywhere — just as the Sages instituted the "Wayfarer's Prayer" for the physical protection of our health and property while we journey. Moshe Rabbeinu did this for Yehoshua, and Calev went to the graves of the forefathers to pray that he be saved from the scheme of the Spies. We, too, can pray that we do not sin when we go about.

(d) Look at your *tzitzis*, as the plain reading of the verse says, "[When] you see them you will remember all of Hashem's commandments and carry them out. And you must not be probing, following you heart and your eyes" (*Bamidbar* 15:39).

CHAPTER NINETEEN

"On That Day Hashem Will Be One"

A. Clarity and Confusion

As we discussed in Chapter Three, the Rishonim understood that the error of idol worship is related to the fact that the world operates under the rule of the officer-angels and the Heavenly bodies — the stars and the zodiac. People knew this fact, but they began to think that these forces had real power, so they began worshiping them and praying to them. Thus the Torah states, "Do not look up toward the heavens, and see the sun, the moon and the stars, the entire heavenly host, and be led astray and bow down to them and serve them — those that Hashem, your God, has assigned for all the nations" (*Devarim* 4:19).[1]

The Rambam (*Hilchos Avodas Kochavim* 1:1) traced their error to the days of Enosh, when they "thought to honor" God's attendants. In other words, they knew that God is the Creator, but they thought that it was proper to serve His attendants as well. Eventually, though, they completely forgot about God, or, at the very least, that God controls all those forces (see above, Chapter Three).

Now, the Ramban (to *Vayikra* 18:25) explains that the type of providence that God uses to govern the world depends on the country: all countries except for the Land of Israel are governed with general providence (through officer-angels), but the Land of Israel is governed with specific providence (by God Himself). He then writes:

> *Outside the Land of Israel, even though everything belongs to the Glorious Name, yet its purity is not perfect, on account of the attendants that rule over it, and the nations stray after their officer-angels to serve them as well.*
> *— Ramban, Vayikra ibid.*

The implication is that outside the Land of Israel it is impossible to see clearly that only God really runs the world. This is also the meaning of the Sages' saying, "Whoever dwells outside the land is akin to one who has no God" (*Kesubos* 110b).

But if clarity is impossible in most of the world, then how are we to understand the verse, "Hear, O Israel: Hashem is our God, Hashem, the One and Only" (*Devarim* 6:4), which Rashi explains to mean: "Hashem, Who is our God, will in the future be universally acknowledged as Hashem, the One and Only God ..., as it is said (*Zechariah* 14:9), 'On that day Hashem will be One and His

---

1. The Ramban discusses this in several places in his commentary to *Chumash*. See, for example, his commentary to *Shemos* 20:2.

Name will be One'" (*Rashi, Devarim* 6:4), and other such statements. After all, the impurity of the other countries should preclude such clarity.

B. A different system for the future

This difficulty, however, can be resolved with the continuation of that Ramban:

> *For this reason Scripture says, "God of all the world will He be called" (Yeshayah 54:5), for He is God over all powers; He rules over everything, and He will in the end "deal with the hosts of the heaven in heaven" (ibid. 24:21), removing the celestial powers and demolishing the array of the attendants, and afterwards He will punish "the kings of the earth on the earth" (ibid.).*
>
> *— Ramban, Vayikra 18:25*

Consequently, the system of general nature — including the use of officer-angels — that had been the cause for the mistake of idolatry will be annulled in the future. At that time the system of specific providence will run the entire world and will be obvious to all. It will then be easy for all the inhabitants of earth to recognize God. This will apparently take place in the days of the Messiah.

C. "The world will run as it always has"

This approach, however, cannot be applied to the opinion of the Rambam, for he writes:

> *Do not think that in the days of the Messiah any of the ways of the world will be annulled, or that there will be anything new in the creation. The world will run as it always has. And though it says in Yeshayah (11:16), "The wolf will live with the sheep and the leopard will lie down with the kid," that is a parable, an allegory. It means that Israel will dwell securely together [even] with nations who*

are compared to a wolf and a leopard.... Likewise, any similar descriptions of the Messianic era are allegories, and in the days of the Anointed King [the Messiah], everyone will understand what the allegory was referring to.
— Rambam, Hilchos Melachim 12:1

The Rambam ruled like the Talmudic sage Shmuel, who said, "The only difference between this world and the days of Messiah is the servitude to the empires" (*Berachos* 34b). Some Sages learned this from the verse, "There is nothing new beneath the sun" (*Koheles* 1:9).

D. Will nature change?

In particular, the Rambam and the Ramban disagree about the future nature of wild animals. According to the Rambam, the verse, "The wolf will live with the sheep" (*Yeshayah* 11:6) should not be understood literally, but as an allegory describing how all the nations will live together in peace. But according to the Ramban (to *Vayikra* 26:6), the verse was meant literally. This disagreement is an echo of the disagreement between the two Sages, Rabbi Yehudah and Rabbi Shimon:

"I will eliminate wild beasts from the land" (Vayikra 26:6). Rabbi Yehudah says, "He will remove them from [the inhabited part of] the world." Rabbi Shimon says, "He will calm them so that they will not cause any harm."
— Sifra, Bechukosai 2:1

The Rambam seems to follow the opinion of Rabbi Yehudah who maintained that in the future God "will remove them from [the inhabited part of] the world," meaning, "wild beasts will not come in their land, for when there is plenitude and an abundance of blessings, and the cities are full of people — beasts do not enter such settled areas" (this is the Ramban's elucidation of Rabbi Yehudah; see *Ramban, Vayikra* 26:6). But the Ramban himself follows the opinion of Rabbi Shimon, that God "will calm them so that they will not cause any harm." That is, "[God] will eliminate the bad [behavior] of the animals from the land. This is the correct interpretation" (*Ramban* ibid.).

Now, according to Rabbi Yehudah, the verse is not describing a change in the nature of the world, for even today wild beasts shun inhabited areas. But according to Rabbi Shimon, Scripture is saying that the world will be different than the way it is now. Will that "new" nature really be without precedent? Not necessarily, as we can see if we read the Ramban carefully:

> *[Rabbi Shimon's] is the correct interpretation, for when the commandments are fulfilled properly, the Land of Israel will be like the world was at its beginning, before the sin of Adam HaRishon, when no beast or reptile would kill a man, just as [the Sages] said, "It is not the wild donkey that kills, but it is sin that kills" (Berachos 33a).... But the beasts of the Land of Israel — when it will be in a state of perfection — will desist from their harmful way, and revert to their original nature with which they were endowed when they were created.... The fulfillment [of this prophecy] will be [in the days of] the Messiah who is destined to come.*
>
> *— Ramban, Vayikra 26:6*

According to this, Rabbi Shimon is not describing "something new beneath the sun," but something that has been forever — before Adam sinned. Similarly, we may say that the "new" system for running the world without the use of officer-angels will also be a reinstating of the system that was used once before (see *Ramban* to *Bereishis* 11:2 and to *Vayikra* 18:25).

E. What will stop people from erring?

Nevertheless, the Rambam differs from the Ramban, for he maintains that nothing will change in the way the world will operate. Our original question, then, stands: If the world will continue to operate in the future as it does now, then how will idolatry be eliminated? What will force the world to acknowledge that it is God alone Who really runs the world?

We must therefore conclude that the Ramban and the Rambam also disagree about the first causes of idolatry. According to the Ramban, idolatry was able to develop because of some spiritual imperfection in the world that automatically made the world a confusing place: "Its purity is not perfect, on account of the attendants that rule over it, and the nations stray after their officer-angels to serve them as well," as the Ramban put it (*Vayikra* 18:25). Consequently, when God will remove the dominion of the upper beings, the purity of the world will be complete and people will no longer err.

But according to the Rambam (at the beginning of *Hilchos Avodas Kochavim*), idolatry began with a minute mistake, with an attempt to honor God through the Heavenly attendants. From there the people spiraled downward all the way to actual idol worship. There is nothing confusing per se about the world, nothing that makes humans inclined to make this error — the ancients simply made a mistake. But in the future it will be impossible to make that mistake again, because in the future "the earth will be as filled with knowledge of Hashem as water covers the seabed," (*Yeshayah* 11:9) and Israel will be a "light to the nations" (ibid. 42:6).

F. The Ravad's argument

Let us delve further into the opinion of the Rambam. He wrote that the verse "The wolf will live with the sheep" (ibid. 11:6) is just an allegory. To this assertion, Ravad countered, "But in the Torah it says 'I will eliminate wild beasts from the land'" (*Vayikra* 26:6), and that verse certainly does not sound like an allegory!

The Radvaz (R' David ibn Zimra) defends the Rambam's position by saying that just as "the wolf will live with the sheep" is an allegory, so too "I will eliminate wild beasts from the land" is an allegory. This is a weak answer, however, because while it is reasonable to say that the verse "the wolf will live with the sheep" is an allegory — it is part of a passage of consolations that can all be interpreted allegorically — it is difficult to say that "I will eliminate wild beasts from the land" is an allegory, because all the other verses in that passage are blessings that are meant literally. Why should we think that just this one verse is not literal?

Furthermore, if the verse "I will eliminate wild beasts from the land" is an allegory saying that no nation will war with them, then the verses are redundant, for the topic of wars is written explicitly in the continuation of that passage: "and no armed forces will pass through your land. You will pursue your enemies and they will fall before you by the sword. Five of you will pursue a hundred [of the enemy], and a hundred of you will pursue ten thousand, and your enemies will fall before you by the sword" (*Vayikra* 26:6-8).

G. Rambam vs. Ravad; Rabbi Yehudah vs. Rabbi Shimon

But there is another way we can understand why the Rambam was not troubled with the verse "I will eliminate wild beasts from the land." As we concluded in section D, the Rambam follows the opinion of Rabbi Yehudah, that "I will eliminate wild beasts from the land" means that they will be naturally eliminated from populated areas — as they are nowadays. Scripture would then be saying that in the future there will be blessing everywhere. The Ravad, on the other hand apparently understood the verse as the Ramban did (following Rabbi Shimon), that it is foretelling a time when the beasts' violent nature will be uprooted. In that case, a wolf could very well live alongside a sheep!

H. Literal in the Land of Israel, allegorical elsewhere

Finally, the Radvaz himself suggests another resolution to the two verses:

> *The proper approach [to this topic] is that the verse ["The wolf will live with the sheep"] is meant literally in the Land of Israel, as is written, "They will neither injure not destroy in all of My sacred mountain; for the land will be filled with knowledge of Hashem..." (Yeshayah 11:9) —*

the known land, [Israel]. Likewise, the verse "I will eliminate wild beasts from the land" [is literal in the Land of Israel]. But in other countries "the world will run as it always has," and the verses are allegories [for other countries, expressing the idea that] "Nation will not lift sword against nation and they will no longer study warfare" (ibid. 2:4). But in the Land of Israel, both the simple meaning and the allegory will be fulfilled. Blessed is the One Who knows the truth! Even our master, [the Rambam,] did not say conclusively that the verses are [only] allegorical, for he wrote, "in the days of the Anointed King [the Messiah], it will become known to all what the allegory was referring to."

— Radvaz to Rambam, Hilchos Melachim 12:1

The approach of the Radvaz is actually quite similar to that of the Ramban, for the Ramban also made the distinction between the Land of Israel and other countries:

According to Rabbi Shimon, who says that [God] will prevent the [beasts] from causing harm, the verse is saying: "and I will eliminate the bad [behavior] of the animals from the land." This is the correct interpretation, for when the commandments are fulfilled properly, the Land of Israel will be like the world was at its beginning, before the sin of Adam HaRishon, when no beast or reptile would kill a man.

— Ramban, Vayikra 26:6

I. Shmuel's proof

As we will see from a careful reading of the Rambam's comments, the Rambam also draws a distinction between the Land of Israel and other countries.

In section C above, we saw that the source for the Rambam's opinion that "the world will run as it always has" is a statement by the Talmudic sage Shmuel. Let us now examine Shmuel's statement and his source.

Shmuel maintained that "the only difference between this world and the days of Messiah is the servitude to the empires, as is written (*Devarim* 15:11), 'For there will not cease to be destitute people within the land.'" (*Berachos* 34b). How does this verse prove that there will be no other changes in nature or in the course of the world? Rashi explains: "'There will not cease to be ...' implies never. Consequently, there will always be wealth and poverty. You may deduce from this that the consolations of the prophets — such as 'There will no longer be any merchants' (*Zechariah* 14:21) — could not have been prophesied for the days of the Messiah, for those [days] are from this world, and [if those prophecies were about the days of the Messiah,] then destitute people will cease" (*Rashi, Shabbos* 63a). In short, since there will be poor people even during the Messianic era, then it must be that nature will not have changed.

Shmuel's teaching also appears in Tractate *Shabbos* (151b). There, too, the topic is poverty:

> *It is taught: Rabbi Shimon ben Elazar says, "Do [charitable acts] even before you find [someone who can receive them]; while you still have [the money]; and while you are still in your own hands [i.e. before you die]." Thus Shlomo, in his wisdom, said, "So remember your Creator in the days of your youth, before the evil days come" (Koheles 12:1) — these are the days of old age; "and those years arrive of which you will say, 'I have no interest in them'" — these are the days of the Messiah, when there will be neither merits nor faults [i.e. "there will be 'neither merits' because there will be no way to gain merit since everyone will be wealthy; 'nor faults' for there will be no way to harden one's heart and close one's hand" (Rashi)]. This differs with Shmuel, for Shmuel said, "The only difference between this world and the days of Messiah is the servitude to the empires, for it is written (Devarim 15:11), 'For there will not cease to be destitute people within the land.'"*
>
> *— Shabbos 151b*

Both of these sources indicate that the main subject of Shmuel's teaching was poverty, which he expanded to apply to other present-day hardships, such as wars. The application of Shmuel's teaching to wars is found elsewhere in Tractate *Shabbos*:

> *Mishnah: A man should not go out [on Shabbos] with a sword or bow… and if he does go out he is liable for the sin-offering. Rabbi Eliezer says: They are ornaments for him. But the Sages say: They are a disgrace, as is written, "They will beat their swords into plowshares and their spears into pruning hooks; nation will not lift sword against nation and they will no longer study warfare" (Yeshayah 2:4).*
>
> *Gemara: It was taught: [The Sages] said to Rabbi Eliezer, "Since they are ornaments for him, why should they cease in the days of the Messiah?" He said to them, "Because they will not be needed, as is written 'nation will not lift sword against nation' [and once they will have no practical use, they will stop being ornaments]." This [statement] disagrees with [the statement of] Shmuel, for Shmuel said, "The only difference between this world and the days of the Messiah is the servitude to the empires, as is written (Devarim 15:11), 'For there will not cease to be destitute people within the land.'" This supports Rabbi Chiya bar Abba, for Rabbi Chiya bar Abba said, "All the prophets prophesied only for the days of the Messiah, but as for the World to Come — 'The eye has never seen [it] except for You, O God'" (Yeshayah 64:3), [and even the prophets did not have the power to see it (Rashi)].*
>
> *— Shabbos 63a*

Rashi explains that Rabbi Eliezer's assertion that weapons will not be needed in the Messianic era disagrees with Shmuel, for Shmuel maintains that they will not cease in the days of the Messiah just like poverty will not cease.

> *Others say: [The Sages] said to Rabbi Eliezer, "Since they are ornaments for him, why should they cease in the days*

of the Messiah?" He said to them, "Indeed, even in the days of the Messiah they will not cease [being weapons]. This is the same as Shmuel's [view].
— Shabbos 63a

According to Shmuel, then, warfare and poverty will continue even in the days of the Messiah.

J. A difficulty with Shmuel's proof

But let us examine the *Chumash* for the context of the verse cited by Shmuel:

> *However, there will be no destitute person among you, for Hashem will surely bless you in the land that Hashem, your God, is giving you as an inheritance, to take possession of it. [This will be] only if you constantly heed the voice of Hashem, your God, to be careful to carry out all these commandments that I am commanding you today.*
> *— Devarim 15:4-5*

Rashi there comments:

> *But further on [in v. 11] it states, "For there will not cease to be destitute people within the land." [Will there be destitute people or not?] When you do the will of God, the needy will be among the others and not among you; if, however, you do not do the will of God, the needy will be among you.*
> *— Rashi, Devarim 15:4*

The fact that the Jews could be poor if they do not do God's will is also implied in the verse, "[This will be] only if you constantly heed the voice of Hashem" (ibid. v. 5), from which we can infer that if you do not heed the voice of Hashem, there will be destitute people among you. Indeed, throughout that passage, *Targum Yonasan* and *Targum Yerushalmi* consistently interpret phrases such as, "If there is a destitute person among you" (ibid. v. 7) to be talking about "when you do not keep the commandments of the Torah."

A precise reading of the verses confirms the distinction between the Land of Israel and other countries. The verse about the persistence of poverty is written in general terms: "For there will not cease to be destitute people within the land," but it does not specify "among you." However, in the verse, "There will be no destitute person among you," it does specify, "among you."

In short, as long as the Jews keep the commandments of the Torah, there will not be poor among them, but there can still be poor people among other nations.

With the above in mind, we may point out a difficulty in Shmuel's proof. Shmuel proved that there will be no changes in the way the world runs in the days of the Messiah from the verse, "For there will not cease to be destitute people within the land." But, as we have just seen, the verse can very easily be explained as referring to other nations, so how does this verse prove that there will be no changes in the Messianic era?

We will return to this question in section I, but first let us raise a question on the Rambam's position. We will see that both difficulties can be resolved with one answer.

K. Is the Rambam's position self-contradictory?

In Chapter Nine of *Hilchos Teshuvah* the Rambam writes (concerning the blessings and curses in the Torah):

> *[God] promised in the Torah that if we will do [the Torah's precepts] with joy and good spirit and we will constantly meditate on its wisdom, then He will remove all the obstacles that hinder us from keeping it — such as illness, war, famine, and the like. And He will shower upon us all of the good things that encourage us to keep the Torah — such as plenitude, peace, and an abundance of gold and silver — so that we will not need to spend all our days on the needs of the body. Instead, we will remain free to study wisdom and to do the commandments so that we will merit the life in the World to Come. Thus, after promising us the*

blessings of this world, [God] said in the Torah, "It will be a merit for us if we are careful to perform this entire commandment before Hashem" (Devarim 6:25) ... [and, conversely,] "Because you did not serve Hashem, your God, amid gladness and goodness of heart, when everything was abundant, so you will serve your enemies whom Hashem will send against you" (ibid. 28:47-48).

All of those blessings and curses are to be understood with the same approach: if you serve God with joy and you observe His path, then He bestows these blessings upon you and He keeps the curses away from you. You will then be free to become wise in the Torah and engage in its [study], so that you can merit the life of the World to Come. He will give you good in the world that is all good, and you will live long in the everlasting world. You will thus merit two worlds: a good life in this world and life in the World to Come.

This is why all of Israel — their prophets and sages — desired the days of the Messiah, so that they will find respite from the empires that prevent them from properly occupying themselves in Torah and mitzvos, and so that they will have the tranquility [needed for] increasing wisdom — because that way they will merit life in the World to Come. For in the [Messianic era], there will be an abundance of knowledge, wisdom and truth .... [Still,] the ultimate reward and everlasting blessing [will only be in] the World to Come, for "the days of the Messiah" is [only an extension] of this world, and the world will still run as it always has, except that the monarchy will return to Israel. The Sages of old have already said, "The only difference between this world and the days of Messiah is the servitude to the empires."

— Rambam, Hilchos Teshuvah 9:1-2

There is a similar passage in the end of the Rambam's *Hilchos Melachim*:

The Sages and the prophets looked forward to the days of the Messiah not so they would be able to dominate the world and not to rule over the nations; not so that all the nations would elevate them; and not so that they would be able to eat, drink, and be merry — but so that they would be free [to study] the Torah and its wisdom, without taskmasters and opponents, in order to merit the life of the World to Come, as we have explained in the Laws of Repentance.

At that time, there will be neither hunger nor war, neither jealousy nor rivalry, but blessing in great abundance. Delicacies will be available like the dust. And the world's only occupation will be [a drive] to know God.

— Rambam, Hilchos Melachim 12:4-5

The question is: The Rambam seems to contradict himself. On the one hand he rules (in *Hilchos Teshuvah* 9:2) like Shmuel that "The only difference between this world and the days of Messiah is the servitude to the empires," yet Shmuel's source is "For there will not cease to be destitute people within the land," so Shmuel maintains that there will be poor people and wars even in the days of the Messiah. But on the other hand, the Rambam describes the advantage of the Messianic era as being a time of supreme tranquility, with peace and plenitude!

L. One answer

The answer to both this question and the one we raised above (in section J) on Shmuel, is actually quite simple: Shmuel agrees to the distinction between the Land of Israel and other countries, yet the verse "For there will not cease to be destitute people within the land" still proves that the nature of the world will not change and, consequently, the verse "There will no longer be any merchants" (*Zechariah* 14:21), which implies that there won't be any poverty at all in the world must be referring to some other era — the era of the World to Come. Still, during the Messianic era the Land of Israel will enjoy unprecedented peace and prosperity, for the Jews at the time will be keeping the commandments properly.

The Rambam is no longer difficult. Yes, "The world will run as it always has" — in the days of the Messiah hardship and difficulty will persist in the world — but for the Land of Israel and its inhabitants there will be peace. May it be God's will, speedily, and in our days.

M. It's all part of the return of sovereignty to Israel

The resolution we have set forth here is also clear from the Rambam's commentary to the Mishnah:

> *However, the days of the Messiah is the era when monarchy will return to Israel, and they will return to the Land of Israel. That king will be very great, and his royal palace in Zion will augment his name. His fame will spread throughout the nations — he will be more famous than King Shlomo! All the nations will make peace with him and all the countries will serve him on account of his great righteousness and because of the wonders that will be brought about by him. Hashem, may He be exalted, will obliterate anyone who will dare rise against him. All the verses of Scripture attest to his success and our success along with his. This does not mean that nature will fundamentally change from the way it is now, but that the sovereignty will return to Israel. The Sages thus said, "The only difference between this world and the days of Messiah is the servitude to the empires" (Berachos 34b), for in his days there will still be wealthy and poor people, and mighty and weak ones — relative to [each] other. But in those days it will be very easy for people to make a living, so that with minimal effort people will amass great gain. This is the meaning of what [the Sages] said, "The Land of Israel is destined to bring forth cakes and cloaks of fine wool" (Shabbos 30b), because a common expression for one who has ready-to-use items is, "So-and-so found baked bread and cooked food."*
>
> *— Rambam, Commentary to Mishnah Sanhedrin Ch. 10*

Here the Rambam wrote explicitly that the great wealth and tranquility of the Messianic era will not be the result of a change of reality but the result of the blessing that will rest upon the Messiah and those who associate themselves with him in the Land of Israel; "our success" will come not independently but "along with his." Thus, the blessing described by the Rambam in *Hilchos Teshuvah* is really an outgrowth of the return of sovereignty to Israel and the end of the "servitude to the empires."

N. Where do they differ?

If the Rambam agrees that the Land of Israel will be blessed, and the Ramban agrees that the other countries outside the land will not function differently in the days of the Messiah, then where do the Rambam and Ramban differ?

They differ with regard to nature itself: The Ramban maintains that the world will return to its original, pre-Sin state, and so animals will change their current nature; but the Rambam maintains that the natural world as we know it will not change whatsoever.

CHAPTER TWENTY

Exile and Redemption

A. Redemption — only after repentance

What must happen before the final Redemption takes place? We will examine a few sources that, at first, seem to contradict each other, but when resolved will give us a more comprehensive view of that era. The Ramban on *Chumash* writes:

> *Know and understand that these curses allude to the first exile, for all the elements of this covenant — the exile and the redemption from it — occurred in the First Temple....*
>
> *Examine further the subject of the redemption from [the Babylonian exile, and you will see] that He only assures*

> *[Israel] that He will remember the covenant of the Fathers and of the remembrance of the land (Vayikra 26:42), but not that He will pardon their iniquity and forgive their sin and that He will love them once again as of old .... Nor does He state that they will return to Him in complete repentance, but only that "they will confess their iniquity, and the iniquity of their fathers" (ibid. v. 40)....*
>
> *However, the covenant in the book of Devarim alludes to our present exile, and to the redemption by which we will be redeemed from it.... We [therefore] observe that there [in the second covenant] neither the end nor the duration [of the exile] are alluded to, and He made no promises of [automatic] redemption [at a specific time], but He made it dependent only on complete repentance (see Devarim 30:2)....*
>
> *The redemption [mentioned] in that second covenant will be a complete redemption, superior to all [the previous ones]. Thus, the [Torah promises,] "And it will be, when all these things happen to you, the blessing and the curse.... He will do good to you and make you more numerous than your forefathers" (ibid. vs. 1-5).*
>
> *— Ramban, Vayikra 26:16*

The portion of "And it will be, when all these happen to you, the blessing and the curse that I put before you" (*Devarim* 30:1) is clearly speaking of the topic of repentance: "You will then reflect upon [them when you are] among all the nations where Hashem, your God, expelled you. You will return to Hashem, your God, with your whole heart and your entire being" (ibid. vs. 1-2). Understandably, then, the Ramban in his commentary there reiterates what he wrote in *Vayikra*:

> *This portion [is referring to] the future, for all its elements have never yet happened. However, they are destined to happen in the future.... "Hashem, your God, will then remove [the layer over] your heart" (Devarim 30:6); this is in accord with what [the Sages] said (Shabbos 104a),*

"He who comes to purify, they help him." That is, He is assuring you that you will return to Him with your whole heart, and He will help you [do so].
—Ramban, Devarim 30:1-6

The Ramban has made it quite clear that the final Redemption is dependent on repentance. This is also the opinion of the Rambam:

Israel will only be redeemed [from exile] through repentance, and the Torah has promised that Israel is destined to repent at the end of their exile, and then they will be redeemed immediately. Thus it is written, "And it will be, when all these things happen to you.... You will return to Hashem, your God.... Hashem, your God, will then come back" (Devarim 30:1-3).
— Hilchos Teshuvah 7:5

B. Revenge for His sake

But now let us turn to the Ramban's commentary in the portion of *Ha'azinu*:

The Song [of Ha'azinu] further says (in Devarim 32:41) that in the end He will take revenge against His adversaries and He will pay back those who hate Him. The reason [they are considered His enemies and not Israel's] is because whatever evils they did to us was out of their hatred of the Holy One; they hate Israel ... because [Israel] refuses to act like them and, instead, worship the Holy One and they keep His commandments ... as the verse says, "Because for Your sake we are killed all the time" (Tehillim 44:23). Thus it is because of their hatred toward the Holy One that they do all these crimes against us, so they are His adversaries and haters, and it is up to Him to take revenge from them....

Now, there is no condition of repentance and serving [God] in this Song; it is a document attesting only that we

will do many evil deeds, but that He, may He be blessed, will punish us with wrath. Yet He will not blot out our memory, and He will return and He will be appeased. He will collect payment from the enemies with His powerful, great, and mighty sword. He will atone for our sins for the sake of His Name. Thus, this Song is an outright promise of the future redemption, contrary to the heretics' opinion.
— Ramban, Devarim 32:40

This seems to contradict the idea that repentance is the prerequisite for the Redemption. How can we resolve these conflicting teachings?

C. Two stages

The solution is that the Redemption will take place in two stages: the first will be God's revenge, and the second will be the restoration of Israel to its former stature.

The first stage of the Redemption will resemble the redemption from the Egyptian Exile. Of that exile we read: "And I will also carry out judgment on the nation that enslaves [them]" (*Bereishis* 15:14). The Ramban on that verse explains that the reason they deserved to be punished was because they initiated evil schemes to harm Israel (beyond what had been decreed upon Israel). "Thus Yisro said, 'For by the very thing that they plotted against [Israel were they punished]' (*Shemos* 18:11), for it was indeed their evil schemes that brought upon them the great punishments that erased them from the world" (*Ramban, Bereishis* 15:14). The Ramban elsewhere writes:

Scripture wrote at length and mentioned many arguments [in favor of] their redemption: "God heard their cry" (Shemos 2:24); "and God recalled His covenant" (ibid.); "God saw" (ibid. v. 25); "and God paid attention" (ibid.); "for I have paid attention to their pains" (ibid. 3:7) — for even though the term that had been decreed upon them had been completed, they were not worthy of being redeemed, as [the prophet] Yechezkel made plain (see

Yechezkel 20:8). Still, because of the cry, He accepted their prayer in His mercy.

— Ramban, Shemos 2:25

The Jews in Egypt were not worthy of being redeemed because of their sins, as recorded in the *Mechilta*:

> *"They did not listen to Moshe, because of shortness of breath ..." (Shemos 6:9). What person is not happy with good tidings? [If someone is told,] "You have a new son," or "Your master is setting you free from slavery," would he not be happy? So why did they "not listen to Moshe"? Because it was hard for them to pull away from idol worship. For it is written, "And I said to them, 'Every man, cast away the detestable [idols] of his eyes; do not defile yourselves with the idols of Egypt'" (Yechezkel 20:7), and it says, "But they rebelled against Me and did not want to listen ... So I acted for the sake of My Name, that it not be desecrated ..." (ibid. vs. 8-9). Thus it is written, "Hashem then spoke to Moshe and to Aharon and commanded them regarding the Children of Israel" (Shemos 6:13).*
>
> *— Mechilta, Bo §5*

Similarly, during the first stage of the final Redemption, when God will punish His adversaries and those who hate Him, the Holy One will not require "repentance and serving [God]," but "He will atone for our sins for the sake of His Name" (*Ramban, Devarim* 32:40). In fact, the Ramban himself links the Exodus to what we are calling the "first stage of the final Redemption":

> *The reason for [saying] "I will then recall for them the covenant with the earlier [generations]" (Vayikra 26:45) is that I will remember this for them whether they are in the land or outside of it, in the exile alluded to here and in all the generations to come. This is the meaning of "I will then recall for them the covenant ... before the eyes of the nations," for the reason He will do this for them is [actually] for the sake of His Great Name, so that it will not be*

desecrated among the nations. It will not be for their sake, since they will not have repented and their iniquities will not have been forgiven. Our Rabbis thus said [on the verse, "I will not have despised them nor rejected them to completely destroy them [or] to annul My covenant with them, for I am Hashem, their God" (ibid. v. 44)]: "I will not have despised them — in the days of Vespasian. Nor rejected them — in the days of Greece. To completely destroy them [or] to annul My covenant with them — in the days of Haman. For I am Hashem, their God — in the days of Gog and Magog" (Sifra to ibid.).

— Ramban, Vayikra 26:45

From the context of the Ramban's words, we see that "the covenant with the earlier [generations]" that guaranteed that God would sanctify His Name in the world through His beloved Israel — the very covenant by which Israel left Egypt — will remain in effect forever. It will apply to all the exiles and it will apply even if Israel is not worthy. It is because of this covenant that God will first take revenge from all those who harmed the Jews in their exiles.

Israel will then be aroused to complete repentance, which will begin the second stage, and the events described in the Torah portion of *Nitzavim* will then commence:

And it will be, when all these things happen to you .... You will then reflect upon them .... You will return to Hashem, your God, with your whole heart and your entire being .... He will gather you in again from all the nations ... and bring you back to the land .... He will do good to you and make you more numerous than your fore-fathers. Hashem, your God, will then remove [the layer over] your heart.

— Devarim 30:1-6

The process described there climaxes with the nullification of the evil inclination, which will occur with the coming of the Messiah. May all this happen speedily, and in our days.

CHAPTER TWENTY-ONE

I Will Never Despise Them

A. Encouraging signs

And because the Holy One, Blessed is He, does not make signs and wonders in every generation for the eyes of every wicked man or heretic, He therefore commanded us that we should always make a memorial or sign [through such physical mitzvos as tefillin, the Pesach offering, etc.] of that which we have seen with our eyes, and that we should transmit the matter to our children, and their children, and their children to their children, to the generations to come.

— Ramban, Shemos 13:16

The Ramban seems to be saying that the miracles of Egypt were potent enough to sustain Israel's fundamental beliefs for all future generations. But according to this, why did the Sages attach such importance to publicizing the miracles of Purim and Chanukah?[1]

The significance of these miracles is almost certainly not for the sake of the fundamentals of faith. Rather, they impressed upon us that even after we have sinned and have gone into exile, the Holy One has still not withdrawn His love for us. They reminded us that the covenant that He established with the forefathers and with Israel will remain in effect forever. Publicizing these miracles thus reinforces what the Torah has explicitly taught us:

> *I will recall My covenant with Yaakov, and also My covenant with Yitzchak, and I will even recall My covenant with Avraham and take account of the land. But the land will be left abandoned.... And even though [I will bring upon them] these [calamities] when they are in the land of their enemies, I will not have despised them nor rejected them to completely destroy them [or] to annul My covenant with them, for I am Hashem, their God. I will then recall for them the covenant with the earlier [generations] whom I took out of the land of Egypt before the eyes of the nations so as to act for them as God; I am Hashem.*
> — *Vayikra 26:42-45*

Note the order of the verses in this passage: Scripture first says, "I will recall My covenant," then continues, "But the land will be left abandoned." This teaches us that the decree of exile is an outcome of God's love, of "I will recall My covenant." Not "the land will be left abandoned" and yet "I will not despise them," but so that "I will not despise them," for exile comes from love — it corrects and saves us just as a doctor may perform painful procedures to save a person's life.

---

1. see *Berachos* 14a; *Shabbos* 23b; and *Megillah* 3b.

The Yalkut Shimoni elaborates on this passage:

> *"I will not have despised them" — in the days of the Chaldeans, for I provided Daniel, Chananiah, Mishael, and Azaryah for them. "Nor rejected them" — in the days of Media, for I provided Mordechai and Esther for them. "To completely destroy them" — in the days of the Greeks, for I provided Shimon the Righteous for them. "To annul My covenant with them" — in the days of the Romans, for I provided Rebbi and the Sages of the generations for them. "For I am Hashem, their God" — in the future to come, for no nation or tongue will be able to dominate them.*
>
> *— Yalkut Shimoni, Bechukosai §675*

This Midrash enumerated all the four exiles, and it teaches us that the original affection for Israel as "My illustrious son" (see *Shemos* 4:22) remained even after sin and exile. "Beloved are [the Children of] Israel, for they are described as children of the Omnipresent" (*Avos* 3:18). This Midrash assures us that He will redeem us and establish us once again as "a kingdom of nobles and a holy nation" (*Shemos* 19:6).

So, yes, the covenant is forever.

B. Torah will preserve the nation

Let us reflect on this *Yalkut Shimoni*. Why did the Midrash list Shimon the Righteous as the Jews' champion during the reign of the Greeks and not Mattisyahu and his sons? After all, the miracle of Chanukah came about through them and they were the ones who banished the Greeks from Israel. It was they who restored the "monarchy to Israel for more than two hundred years, until the destruction of the Second Temple" (*Rambam, Hilchos Chanukah* 3:1). Furthermore, "They were extremely pious, and if not for them Torah and mitzvos would have been forgotten from Israel" (*Ramban, Bereishis* 49:10). Were they not, then, the guardians of Israel in that era?

There are two possible answers to this question. One answer is based on *Megillah* (11a). There the Gemara records an almost identical Midrash to the one found in *Yalkut Shimoni*, but there, after listing Shimon the Righteous, it does list Mattisyahu and his sons. Perhaps the *Yalkut Shimoni* simply condensed the Midrash.

That, however, is not enough of an answer because we should still wonder why the *Yalkut* chose Shimon the Righteous as the representative of that era and why the Gemara listed him first.

The more complete answer, though, is that Shimon the Righteous lived in the beginning of the Greek era, long before the Chashmonaim; moreover, he was of much greater stature then they because, as one of the survivors of the Great Assembly, he was a central transmitter of the Torah. It was thanks to him that the Torah was preserved, and that Mattisyahu and his sons were inspired enough to fight for the sanctification of God's Name.

The *Yalkut,* however, was not listing all the saviors of Israel but the bearers and guardians of the Torah. Thus the beginning of that *Yalkut* was elaborating on the importance of the Torah for Israel:

> *"I will not have despised them nor rejected them to completely destroy them" — what was left of them that was not despised? After all, all the benefits that were given to them were revoked, so what was left for them? It was the Torah scroll, for if that would not have endured for Israel they would have been no different than the nations.*
>
> *— Yalkut Shimoni, Bechukosai §675*

The *Yalkut* then continues with the section we quoted above, "I will not have despised them — in the days of the Chaldeans," etc. Since the topic of the *Yalkut* was the importance of the Torah for the preservation of Israel, it lists those who were vital to the Torah's transmission in all the exiles, down to Rebbi and the Sages of the later generations.

C. A Purim lesson: "God loves us!"

The Gemara (*Shabbos* 88a) informs us that the Jews "accepted the Torah again in the days of Achashveirosh." Why did they do this? "Because of the love of the miracle that was done for them" (*Rashi* ad loc.). This is puzzling: Were all the wondrous, outright miracles of Egypt not enough reason for them to accept the Torah out of love? Why did they wait for the miracle of Purim?

With what we have discussed here, however, we can answer that this miracle showed the Jews just how much God loves them. They saw that even after they had sinned so much that it was deemed necessary to send them into exile, to destroy the *Beis HaMikdash*, and to remove His *Shechinah* from that place — nevertheless, His love for them remained as steadfast as ever. They saw that, indeed, "I will not have despised them nor rejected them... to annul My covenant with them," and that Haman's decree was designed by God only as a facade that would drive them back to His Torah. Now they were able to see how decrees against them are truly good for them and are what binds His covenant to them.

D. True love

> *Hashem, your God, chose you to be a special people among all the nations on the face of the earth. It was not because you were more numerous than all the other nations that Hashem embraced you and chose you; you are among the smallest of all the nations. It was because of Hashem's love for you, and because He was keeping the oath that He had made to your fathers.*
>
> — *Devarim 7:6-8*

On this, the Ramban comments:

> *The meaning of "Hashem embraced you" is that He tied Himself to you with a firm knot to guarantee that He will never become separated from you.... "And [He] chose you" from among all the nations so that you will be a treasure and inheritance for Him, for the idea of choosing — wherever it appears — means selecting from among others.*

Then [Hashem] said [why He chose you]: "It was because of Hashem's love for you" — that is why He chose you, for He saw that you are worthy of being loved before Him.... He did not [need to] mention any [other] reason for choosing them [other than His love], for the one a lover will choose is someone who will bear the lover and whatever comes from [Him] — and, in this regard, Israel is the most [appropriate choice].
— *Ramban, Devarim 7:6*

What God saw in them, Israel saw in Him. When Israel saw how patient God was with them — despite all they had done against Him — and that His love for them remained so firm that He did the Purim miracle for them — in their enemy's land! — they willingly and lovingly accepted the entire Torah upon themselves. From the Exodus they had already acquired faith, but from Purim they acquired love.

E. God will always love us

Since this lesson is so important, we have collected several sources that describe God's love for us, even in our exile.

Said the Holy One to Israel: "Do not think that I am treating you like a slave whom the master wishes to sell as defective merchandise, at whatever price he can get. Rather, the reason I am bringing hardship upon you is to make you direct your hearts to Me...." To what extent will I chastise you? Down to the heels... until you keep [all of] My commandments down to [your] heels [i.e. even the ones considered insignificant by people].
— *Devarim Rabbah 3:2*

Said Rabbi Acha: The Holy One took an oath that He would never forsake Israel.
— *Ibid.*

For the mountains may be moved and the hills may falter, but My kindness shall not be removed from you and

My covenant of peace shall never falter, said the One Who shows you mercy, Hashem.
— *Yeshayah 54:10*

Thus said Hashem, Who gives the sun as a light by day and the laws of the moon and the stars as a light by night; Who agitates the sea so that its waves roar; Hashem, Master of Legions, is His Name: If these laws could be removed from before Me — the word of Hashem — so could the seed of Israel cease from being a people before Me forever. Thus said Hashem: If the heavens above could be measured or the foundations of the earth plumbed below, so too would I reject the entire seed of Israel because of everything they did — the word of Hashem.
— *Yirmiyah 31:34-36*

Malachi, who was the last of the prophets, and whose words were meant as encouragement for the long exile, opens his book with, "I loved you, says Hashem" (*Malachi* 1:2). Again, in the last chapter he writes: "Behold, I am sending My messenger, and he will clear a path before Me; suddenly the Lord Whom you seek will come to His Sanctuary.... For I, Hashem, have not changed; and you, the sons of Jacob, you have not perished.... Return to Me and I will return to you" (ibid. 3:1-7). The Radak there comments:

But "you have not perished" nor will you ever perish, for you will always be special among the nations, a unique nation in the land. And even though you went into exile and you have been scattered to all ends, still, your mark has remained in all places. Whatever misfortune I have brought upon you was because of your sins. Yet just as I will never change so, too, you will never perish. And in the end of days you will return to your original stature and you will be supreme over all the nations of the earth.
— *Radak, Malachi 3:6*

Malachi then closes his book with these words:

Remember the Torah of Moshe My servant, which I commanded him at Horeb for all of Israel.... Behold, I send you Eliyahu the prophet before the coming of the great and awesome day of Hashem. And he will turn back [to God] the hearts of the fathers with [their] sons and the hearts of sons with their fathers.

— *Ibid. 3:22-24*

Indeed, the covenant of love between God and Israel is everlasting!

CHAPTER TWENTY-TWO

The Purpose of the Creation

A. Hodaah: Acknowledging and giving thanks to God

In Chapter Nine we discussed the idea that the purpose of creation was to give creatures the ability to come to know God. But there is a more advanced level of this concept that can be summarized as acknowledging and giving thanks to God (*hodaah* in Hebrew) It means that once we reach faith and knowledge of God, we must then constantly acknowledge and thank Him for the mighty acts of kindness that He has done for us. The Ramban, among others, taught us this lesson:

[The Sages] therefore said: "Be as scrupulous in performing a 'minor' mitzvah as a 'major' one" (Avos 2:1), for they are all precious and cherished, for through them a person can acknowledge God['s sovereignty] all the time, and the purpose of all the mitzvos is that we should believe in our God and acknowledge that He created us. [Indeed,] this is the purpose of the creation. For we have no other reason for the original creation. And the Almighty has no interest in the lower creatures except so that man should know and acknowledge to his God that He created him. Thus, the purpose for raising our voices in prayer, the purpose in synagogues, and the advantage of public prayer is so that people will have a place to gather to acknowledge to the Almighty that He created them and brought them forth. They will publicize this, and they will declare before Him: "We are your creatures!"
— Ramban, Shemos 13:16

The Ramban makes it clear that giving thanks to God is the goal of all the commandments and the purpose of all of creation. Every mitzvah we do is an act of acknowledgment, as it demonstrates that we recognize the Master Who issued the command. When we do a mitzvah, we are in effect saying that we are His slaves and that He created and sustains us so that we will be able to do his will. Praying — especially public prayer in a synagogue — is the most obvious from of this acknowledgment, for in it we openly declare: "We are Your creatures!"

As we alluded to above, the idea of *hodaah* encompasses both acknowledgment and thanksgiving (as in praising and singing to God).[1] We have just seen that mitzvos express our acknowledgment of God. Do they also express praise of God? Yes, they do, as we learn from the following Gemara: "'The dead cannot praise God' (*Tehillim* 115:17). The following is what [David] really meant to say: A person should occupy himself with [the study of] Torah and [the practice of] mitzvos before he dies, for once he

1. [For a discussion of the conceptual connection between acknowledgement and thanksgiving, see *Pachad Yitzchak, Chanukah, Maamar* II - ed.]

dies, he is idled from [the study of] Torah and [the practice of] mitzvos; and then the Holy One no longer gains any praise from him" (*Shabbos* 30a). This Gemara explicitly equates exertion in Torah and mitzvos with giving praise to God.

B. All mitzvos are praises

Rabbi Meir used to say, "There isn't a single Jew who is not surrounded by [seven] mitzvos: tefillin on his head, tefillin on his arm, a mezuzah at his door, and four tzitzis surrounding him. About these David said, 'Seven times a day I have praised You'" (Tehillim 119:164).
— Tosefta, Berachos 6:25

From this *Tosefta*, as well, we see that merely doing the action of a mitzvah is considered giving praise to God. The fact that the *Tosefta* only lists "testimonial" and "memorial" commandments does not mean that non-verbal praise of God is limited to these mitzvos, because once we see that it is possible to praise God using action alone, we know that we don't have to say a word to praise Him — and this applies to all mitzvos.

C. The duty of all creatures

"For such is the duty of all the creatures" (*Shacharis* for Shabbos) — all creatures were created to praise God. Our Sages said:

The Holy One created heaven and earth so that they would praise Him. What is the source? The verse, "The heavens declare the glory of God" (Tehillim 19:2). But when Moshe came, he silenced them, as is written, "Listen carefully, heavens, and I shall speak" (Devarim 32:1).
— Devarim Rabbah 10:2

Said Rabbi Meir: The Angel of Death went to Moshe, and told him, "The Holy One sent me to you, for you will depart on this day." Moshe replied, "Go away, for I wish to praise the Holy One." How do we know this? For it is written, "I shall not die! But I shall live and relate the deeds of

God" (Tehillim 118:17). [The Angel of Death] said to him, "Moshe, why are you being so haughty? [God] has others who can praise him — heaven and earth praise him all the time...." Moshe said to him, "[True,] but I silence them and I praise Him, as is written, 'Listen carefully, heavens, and I shall speak'" (Devarim 32:1).
— Devarim Rabbah 11:5

When Scripture said, "From the rising of the sun to its setting, Hashem's Name is praised" (Tehillim 113:3), [it means,] from the time the sun rises until it sets, it praises the Holy One. You likewise find that when Yehoshua stood up at Givon and wanted to silence the sun, he did not say, "Sun, stand still ['amod'] at Givon," but, "Sun, stand silent ['dom'] at Givon" (Yehoshua 10:12), because as long as [the sun] travels it praises the Holy One, and as long as it praises, it has power to exist. Yehoshua therefore told it, "Stand silent," [so that it would stop moving].
— Yalkut Shimoni, Yehoshua §22

The Midrash implies that the sun actually praises God, not metaphorically — by traveling through the sky — but literally — it sings to God! Thus the verses, "Praise Hashem from the heavens; praise Him in the heights: Praise Him all His angels; praise Him, all His legions. Praise Him sun and moon; praise Him, all bright stars.... Praise Hashem from the earth: sea giants and all watery depths; fire and hail ... the mountains ... and the beasts ..." (*Tehillim* 148:1-10) — can all be understood literally, according to the plain reading of the words. This Midrash is clear proof for the Rambam's opinion:

All the planets and all the stars are beings that possess souls, insight and intellect; they are alive and enduring; and they recognize the One Who spoke and the world came into being. Each and every one — in accord with its size and stature — praises and glorifies its Creator, just like the angels.
— Rambam, Hilchos Yesodei HaTorah 3:9

D. Inspiration for people

The Rambam, however, does distinguish between the heavenly bodies and the elements. Concerning the four classical elements — fire, wind, water, and earth — he writes:

> *These four entities do not possess a soul, do not know, and have no awareness; rather, they are like lifeless corpses. And each one has a routine which it cannot alter and of which it is not even aware. Thus David said, "Praise Hashem from the earth: sea giants and all watery depths; fire and hail, snow and vapor" (Tehillim 148:7-8). This means, "People, praise Him because of His mighty deeds that you see [embodied] in fire, hail, and in the other creatures that are observable beneath heaven. For the power of these things is readily seen by big and small alike.*
>
> *— Rambam, Hilchos Yesodei HaTorah 3:11*

According to the Rambam, then, each part of the psalm must be understood separately, in accord with its topic and context: the luminaries, which do have inherent intelligence, sing to God for themselves; but the other creatures, which do not have intelligence, "sing" to God by being the inspiration for humans to praise God for His wondrous deeds.

E. The song of Torah

Another source supporting the Rambam's position is found in *Midrash HaNeelam:*[2]

> *The sun rises from below the earth and reaches the point [in the sky] known as karbosa in Greek. From that point it begins to climb higher and higher, and the sound that it [makes] in its journey is heard in all the heavens, [calling] everything to join in the song that it is chanting. No human heard its voice except for Moshe, who*

2. This Midrash is otherwise known as *Zohar* Chadash. The reference numbers given here are the way they appear in the Sulam edition of the *Zohar.*

was faithful to the King, and Yehoshua, who was [Moshe's] attendant.
— *Midrash HaNeelam, Bereishis §622*

Now, there are verses that seem to say that trees, plants, and other inanimate objects do sing to God, but the Midrash teaches that all those verses are not referring to any observable objects in our universe, but to sublime matters that exist in the upper realms:

> *We have learned: When the Northern wind blows at midnight, and the Holy One enters Gan Eden, all the fragrant plants and all the trees in Gan Eden give forth their fragrance and they sing before Him, as is written, "Then all the trees of the forest will sing with joy — before Hashem" (I Divrei HaYamim 16:33).... And all the tzaddikim delight in the supernal glow, and they are nourished by it, so they sing before their Creator in Gan Eden. Thus it is written, "Let my Beloved come to His garden and eat its precious fruit" (Shir HaShirim 4:16).*
> — *Midrash HaNeelam, Bereishis §544-545*

Meaning, when my Beloved comes to His garden, He will "eat" those who are waiting for him — and who are they? The "precious fruit" — the *tzaddikim.*

The Midrash continues:

> *The Sages taught: When the Northern wind begins to blow, the whole sky, all the heavens, the Chayos-angels, the Ofanim, and the entire heavenly host — all shudder and shake. Then they break out in glad song and praises to the One Who spoke and the world came into being, until He goes into Gan Eden together with the tzaddikim. This is at midnight.*
>
> *Said Rav Yehudah in the name of Rav: Whoever has a holy soul within him, and hears the sound of the rooster crowing at midnight... [which is when] the Holy One enters Gan Eden... and has understanding in his heart, rouses himself and gets up to study the Torah. His voice*

> *goes forth and is heard in Gan Eden, and the Holy One listens. Whereupon the tzaddikim say to Him, "Master of the Universe! Who is this person?" and He answers, "It is So-and-so, and the holy soul that is within him is engrossed in studying the Torah. All of you, listen! for I prefer this to all the songs and praises that the [angels] say up above."*
> *— ibid. §546-548*

The Gemara, as well, describes Torah study as a "song." Reish Lakish said, "Whoever engages in the Torah by night, the Holy One extends a thread of grace upon him by day, for it is written (*Tehillim* 42:9), 'In the day, Hashem will command His kindness.' And why does Hashem command His kindness by day? Because 'by night, I will sing to Him'" (*Chagigah* 12b).

F. Parallel praises

So far, we have seen that there are creatures in Heaven that sing to God and there are creatures on earth that praise Him. The Midrash tells us that there is a unity and correspondence among all those that praise God:

> *Said Rabbi Yehoshua ben Levi in the name of Rabbi Yochanan: The Holy One made ministering angels above so that they would sing praises and extol Him. They sing hymns and glad songs before Him, every single day.*
>
> *And we learned: The night is divided into three watches, and there are three groups of angels — one for each of these three watches — who praise the Creator in each of the watches. Corresponding to these [three watches] there are three prayers in every day, at which Israel gathers to praise their Creator.*
> *— Midrash HaNeelam, Bereishis §752-753*

G. The song of Shabbos

There is a special time of each week most suited for praising God. That day is Shabbos, as the Midrash teaches:

Said Rabbi Yehudah in the name of Rav: The Holy One did not sit on the Throne of His Glory until Shabbos came, and then He went up and sat on His throne. Rabbi Yose said to him, "But did He not sit even before the world was created — He was, He is, and He will be!" Said Rabbi Yehudah... [what this means is,] before the world was created, there was no one to praise Him, or even recognize Him, but once he created the world — He created angels and the holy Chayos-angels, heaven and all its hosts, and he created Man. All of them were ready to praise their Creator and glorify Him, yet the glory and the praise did not come before Him until Shabbos began. Then they all became silent, and they broke out into glad singing and praises — the upper [creatures] together with the lower [creatures], and then He sat on the Throne of His Glory. That is to say, then there were creatures who recognized His honor and praised it.

Rabbi Yehudah further said: There is no greater praise and exaltation before the Holy One like the praise of Shabbos — when the upper creatures and the lower creatures all praise Him in unison. And even the Shabbos day itself praises him. Thus it is written, "A psalm, a song for the Shabbos day" (Tehillim 92:1).

— Midrash HaNeelam, Bereishis §722-724

The Sages apparently formulated the special pre-*Shema* prayer of Shabbos morning to correspond to this Midrash. The prayer reads:

All the host above bestows praise on Him, splendor and greatness — the Seraphim, Chayos, and holy Ophanim — to the God Who rested from all works, Who on the Seventh Day was elevated and sat on the Throne of His Glory.... And the Seventh Day gives praise saying: "A psalm, a song for the Shabbos Day" (Tehillim 92:1).

— Shacharis for Shabbos

Siddur HaGra indeed notes the above quoted *Zohar* as the source for this prayer.

H. Singing is the highest form of Divine worship

Of all the forms of Divine worship, singing and praising God are the highest ones. Singing is the service performed by the angels; it was the important service performed by the Levites in the *Beis HaMikdash*; and it was the service of all the Jews who had gathered in the Courtyard of the Beis HaMikdash to bring their *Pesach*-offerings — there they would recite *Hallel*, with feelings of wondrous, holy exultation.

I. Ruach hakodesh and true song

The songs that are truly desired for Divine service are the ones that flow from a *ruach hakodesh* (spirit of holiness) that comes upon a person. For example, the Sages taught regarding the Song of the Sea that "the Divine spirit rested upon them so they sang" (*Shemos Rabbah* 23:2). Or, as the Midrash quoted above in section E said, "All of the *tzaddikim* delight in the supernal glow, and they are nourished by it, so they sing before their Creator in Gan Eden." With this in mind, we can understand the Gemara that describes the return of the Ark from the Philistines (see *I Shmuel* Ch. 6). The Philistines had placed the Ark on a wagon pulled by two cows, and "the cows set out on the direct road [*vayisharna*]" (ibid. v. 12). The Gemara asks: "What does '*vayisharna*' mean? Said Rabbi Yochanan in the name of Rabbi Meir: 'They sang [*shirah*]'" (*Avodah Zarah* 24b). Why would cows sing? How could they? Rather, they were carrying the Ark of Hashem — where the Divine Presence is manifest — so they recited song. Perhaps the Divine Presence was especially felt at that time because there was an extra measure of holy joy in the world, for the Ark was being returned to His children, Israel.

The connection between *ruach hakodesh* and praising God also sheds light on the esoteric idea that on Shabbos much of the universe joins to praise God (see above, G), and even the Shabbos day itself praises God: Shabbos is a day of intense holiness, so the Divine spirit permeates creation that much more.

Knowing God is the source of life, therefore:

> *The angels subsist on the glow of the Shechinah. And so the [Sages] expounded: "'You give them all life [m'chayeh]' (Nechemia 9:6) — 'You are the sustenance [michya] of them all' (Shemos Rabbah 32:4). And of [the glow of the Shechinah] it is written, 'Sweet is the light' (Koheles 11:7), since they perceive a good 'flavor' in the light."*
>
> — *Ramban, Shemos 16:6*

Therefore, any song that expresses thanksgiving to God, that flows out of a recognition of God, will fortify and maintain life. This idea is captured in the following Midrash:

> *"Then I said, 'Woe is me, for I was silent [nidmeisee]'" (Yeshayah 6:5). [The prophet Yeshayah] saw the ministering angels praising the Holy One, but he did not join his praise with theirs. He then became upset, [and he said,] "for I am a man of impure lips and I dwell among a people with impure lips," for had I joined my praises to theirs, I would have lived forever just like them.*
>
> — *Yalkut Shimoni, Yeshayah §406*

Moreover, through song and praises of God, people attain life in the World to Come, as is written, "Awake and sing joyfully, you who rest in the dirt" (*Yeshayah* 26:19).

> *Rabbi Meir said: What is the source in the Torah for the Resurrection of the Dead? It is written, "Then Moshe and the Children of Israel will sing this song to Hashem" (Shemos 15:1). It does not say "sang" but "will sing"; from here we see that the [concept of] the Resurrection of the Dead is found in the Torah.*[3]
>
> — *Sanhedrin 91b*

---

3. The topic of the Resurrection of the Dead is discussed in *Sanhedrin* 90b-92b.

Thus song maintains life, intensifies life, and — in the future — will restore life.

Song expresses acknowledgment of God and, at the same time, it reinforces that recognition. Of Shabbos, which is a miniature of the World to Come, it is written: "May Your children recognize and know that from You comes their rest, and through their rest, they will sanctify Your Name."

This volume is part of
THE ARTSCROLL SERIES®
an ongoing project of
translations, commentaries and expositions
on Scripture, Mishnah, Talmud, Halachah,
liturgy, history, the classic Rabbinic writings,
biographies and thought.

For a brochure of current publications
visit your local Hebrew bookseller
or contact the publisher:

Mesorah Publications, ltd
4401 Second Avenue
Brooklyn, New York 11232
(718) 921-9000
www.artscroll.com